CW00418403

The First Diana.
The Tragic Story of Lady Diana Spencer
Almost a Princess.

by

Sarah J Freeman

Sarah J Freeman

We are such stuff as
dreams are made on;

and our little life is
rounded with a sleep.

William Shakespeare.

Sarah J Freeman

TABLE OF CONTENTS

License Notes

This Book is licensed for personal enjoyment only. It may not be resold or given away to others. If you wish to share this book, please purchase an additional copy. If you are reading this book and it was not purchased then, you should purchase your own copy. Your continued respect for author's rights is appreciated.

Chapter One

1735

Diana's bedroom at Southampton House was large and sumptuously decorated. Despite her illness and the weakness that it brought down upon her, she could still appreciate the beauty of her surroundings.

The room was warm and there were many velvets which, regardless that spring was turning into summer, Diana was grateful for. She seemed to feel the cold perpetually and was only warmed when seized by one of her more violent fits of coughing.

Diana's four-poster bed was immense and the ceiling of her room so very high that the drapes which hung down all around her seemed almost as long green velvet shields against the world.

The green was somewhere between the colour of faded limes and summer grass and something about the shade made Diana think of health and well-being.

Although there were hints of that same colour here and there about the room, the rest was a rather nice mixture of creams and gold. The walls were panelled in oak which had been painted in a rich ivory colour, and the small footstools and chairs had been upholstered in a rich golden velvet. The great curtains at the windows, although in a shade of green identical to her bed canopy drapes, were neatly fastened with great rope-like and tasselled golden sashes.

The great open fireplace was so wide that Diana had often thought she could easily lay down in it and, as tall as she was, never touch either end with her head or her toes. A maid seemed almost to continually check upon the fire adding logs and coals to keep it roaring and her mistress good and warm. The maid would certainly not let Diana Russell, the Duchess of Bedford, get cold and sicker still.

In the far corner of the room, beneath the great window through which daylight poured, there was a beautiful walnut writing desk. However, since Diana had arrived at Southampton House, she had not even had the strength to sit up straight in her chair, never mind being able to write. Instead, a maid had fetched in a simple writing tray for her to use whilst still maintaining the comfort and warmth of her own bed. It was from just that position that she set about writing a long letter to her grandmother, the Dowager Duchess of Marlborough. Diana had not seen her grandmother since she had been moved from Woburn Abbey to Southampton House in Bloomsbury Square in London by her husband.

Diana could not help but smile to herself; the move had only taken place because her formidable grandmother had demanded it. The Dowager Duchess of Marlborough nearly always got what is was that she wanted.

My Dear Grandmother,

I am now arrived at Southampton House and would beg that you come to me as soon as you are able. As wonderful as it is here in our London home, I cannot help but wish that I could make the journey across town to Marlborough House and stay with you. In many ways, it would make me feel as though I had never left you and that you and I had never been parted.

Oh, I would say that it was true, my dear Grandmother. How I wish the last years had never happened and that I was still no more than a girl living in your beautiful home and writing your letters for you.

Still, if you come to me at Bloomsbury Square that shall, at least, make me feel so very much better.

My health does not improve, Grandmother, and I found the journey from Bedfordshire down to London rather more arduous than ever I have done before. It was as if I could feel every dent in the pock-marked road, almost as if I were being rolled along it in my own person rather than being driven along it in my husband's finest carriage. It brought on several coughing fits, all of which seemed to displease John greatly. It is as if he has little time or sympathy for my illness. I am sure he is in the full belief that I have somehow brought the thing upon myself; that I have somehow worked to make my illness manifest.

My husband serves me well, does he not? But perhaps I should not make jokes or be so scathing. And yet, I cannot help it. I do not feel as well disposed to the Duke as once I did. He has become less and less attentive over the time I have been here and, already, he has made his way back to Woburn Abbey on the idea that he has something he must attend to in the immediate. He did not say what and I did not ask. I rather fear I have become that sort of a wife; an unquestioning wife.

You would never have been such, would you, my dear Grandmother? You have been blessed with the sort of strength and determination which would serve me well at this moment. If only I could search my being and find an ounce of what resides in your own spirit.

I continue to lose weight, Grandmother, and have diminished further, even since I last saw you at Woburn Abbey. The more I continue to cough and spit blood the more I begin to fear that the doctors are right. I truly am suffering from tuberculosis. I did not quite believe it at first. I daresay the truth is that I did not want to believe it.

Still, I must take care to be optimistic about things. It is true that many people survive this dreadful illness. Consumption is not now a death sentence, and I must not dare to think of it as such. It is just so difficult when I am feeling at my worst, too weak to even stand.

What pains me more than anything, what hurts me more than any physical ailment, is the idea that I am now certain that I no longer carry a baby. The morning sickness is long gone if it ever truly was morning sickness, and I have suffered enough these last two days to know that I cannot possibly be carrying a child any longer.

I have yet to say anything of this to John. As you know, the Duke blames me for the loss of our last unborn child and has kept up such a countenance on the matter these last two years. I fear I should not have mentioned a thing to him when first I thought myself to be with child again. But, you see, I thought it would cheer him and therefore cheer us both. These two years have been a wilderness of sadness and suffering, and I would have given anything to have the power to change it all right here inside my own wasting body. And yet, that is the cause, is it not? My body is wasting, and wasting day by day. No child could be conceived within this husk of a human being and yet hope to survive.

Of course, the day shall come when I shall have to tell it all to John. I shall have to tell him soon that, once again, I have lost his heir.

If only he were not a Duke. If only he were an ordinary man and I an ordinary woman. Perhaps then he could simply comfort me and feel sad only for the loss of his child; a human being in the making. Instead, we have the weight of duty and expectation everywhere, and it makes us so that we cannot comfort one another. In truth, we are a torment to one another. He torments me with his disappointment and expectation, and I torment him with my inability to produce his heir. But of course, we are not ordinary, and I know that you would never have us so. You strove so hard to ensure that my life was anything but ordinary, and I should not offend you by wishing things to truly be otherwise.

I know how hard you have worked and how much you have sacrificed to give me a life that was anything but ordinary. In truth, my life has been so very crowded with incidents that I should feel nothing but blessed by it all. And yet, there is this terrible hole; this gaping chasm that no adventure or luxury could ever fill.

Oh, Grandmother, I feel so dreadfully unwell that I fear I might never, ever be a mother. With just weeks until I reach five and twenty years of age and three failed attempts,

I fear my womanly destiny shall never be fulfilled.

How cross you would be with me if you were here now. How much you would scold me, my dear Grandmother, for lying about in so much self-pity. And I would welcome your wonderful scorn, for it would make me feel alive again. It would give me the fight I need; however much blood I cough into my handkerchiefs and however lethargic I am prone to feel.

Now that I am here in London, please come to see me as often as you can. I find it so hard to write, and I fear I shall never manage to keep up our correspondence of two or three long letters every week. I cannot yet sit at my writing table and am forced to sit propped upon my pillows with a tray on my lap. I began to fall into sleep whilst writing my last letter and did spill my small dish of ink all over the linens and my nightgown. Still, my maids here are so very kind and attentive that they begin to feel like friends. But that should not be the case, should it? My husband should be here at my side; my husband ought really to be my friend, did he not? I always thought a husband should be to me just what your husband was to you. Grandfather was the most devoted of men, was he not? I still miss him these thirteen years later and wish with all my heart that he could have been spared. What a formidable pair you made together, and how you must miss him, Grandmother. You had more than forty years of happiness with your husband, and yet, after less than four years of matrimony, I cannot imagine the same will be true of myself, even if the Good Lord does spare me and carry me through this dreadful malady.

I shall be here alone for the next several days with the Duke back in Bedfordshire so you might care to make several visits. I know that you no longer have an easy relationship with my husband and you might find it easier to come to me now whilst he is departed. Not that you would ever have waited any man's say so before coming to me. Nay, not in any single thing would you ever have been thwarted, my good and strong Grandmother, by any mere man. You have known royalty and politics and war, and you have known well how to deal with each and every one of them. What a wonderful influence you have had in the world, and a world where men think they hold all the keys and even more of the answers. How very proud I am to be your Granddaughter. I wonder if Grandfather would ever have dared to say the things to you that my husband has said to me. No, and nor would they have entered his head. Grandfather was full of love and devotion. My husband is not.

As I have lain upon my sick bed for so many weeks, I have begun to think back over my life. For one such as yourself, you might say that I have not yet lived long enough to truly deserve to wallow in such reminiscences. You might well be right. And yet, I cannot help but drift back in time.

It is as if I want to escape back into a time when I was happier, and I felt safe, with no weight of duty or responsibility upon my narrow shoulders.

And yet, the past was not so free of pain and regret, was it? As I lay here and think to my earliest memories, a childhood of running and playing and squealing around the soft and lush green lawns of Althorpe, I am soon cut to the quick. I run and play in my mind, and then the first of my tragedies comes upon me. My six-year-old self ceases in her running and squealing, and it all turns into tears and anguish.

Forgive me, Grandmother, for this is

how I have been these past days. Perhaps once I have seen your beautiful face and intelligent eyes I shall find myself much improved in health as well as in spirit.

With every loving thought,

Your Little Di.

Sarah J Freeman

Chapter Two

With her letter sealed and dispatched, Diana Russell knew it would not be long before her grandmother arrived. The letter would be with her at Marlborough House before the sun had gone down and Diana knew well that the Dowager Duchess of Marlborough would arrive at her bedside the very next day.

That was how things had always been between Diana and her grandmother. Sarah Churchill, the Dowager Duchess, was not a character that everyone could claim to like or have sympathy with. In truth, she was rather harsh when she needed to be and always spoke her mind, even when it was not prudent to do so. Perhaps, sometimes, *because* it was not prudent to do so. It always rather struck Diana that her grandmother enjoyed to be at odds with others; she liked the confrontation of it all. More than anything, she liked to be right.

And yet there had come a day when a six-year-old Diana had seen the chink in the armour of the formidable woman who was her grandmother.

In the Spring of 1716, Lady Anne Spencer, Diana's mother, had died. At only three and thirty years, she left behind five children; Robert, aged fifteen, Anne, aged fourteen, Charles, aged ten, John, aged eight, and Diana, aged just six years.

"But where has Mama gone?"

"Oh, Di, Mama has died. Mama has gone to Heaven." Anne took her little sister into her arms.

Charles and John were so young, yet just

old enough to understand entirely what had happened. Diana was not, she was confused and hurt, almost betrayed at her mother's absence.

"I know that, Anne. But when is Mama coming back?"

"Dear little Di, Mama is not coming back to us. We shall not see her again until we go to Heaven ourselves one day."

"Is that really true, Anne? Is Mama really not ever coming back? Does Papa know about this? Have you told him?" Tears rolled down her chubby pink cheeks.

"Papa already knows, Di," Anne said, holding back tears of her own. But, with so many little ones below her and a father who could do nothing to comfort any of them, Anne had to maintain an orderly set to her own emotions.

"But Papa does not cry. Charles and John are crying, but Papa is not."

"I know, but men do not allow themselves to cry at such things. They do not allow themselves to cry at anything."

"But Robert is crying, Anne." Diana looked miserably over at her eldest brother.

"He is but fifteen, Di. Robert is allowed to cry too." Anne lifted Diana off her feet and held her tightly in her arms.

Diana Spencer sobbed hard, the realisation that she would never see her Mama again starting to sink in. As she sobbed and dangled helplessly in her older sister's arms, she saw her father pass through the drawing-room.

Charles Spencer, the Earl of Sunderland, looked vaguely at his distressed children.

Seeing that Anne and a number of female household staff were doing the lion's share of the consoling, he continued on through the room without stopping to speak to any of them. His ordinarily round face looked grey and suddenly gaunt against the murky whiteness of his wig. His clothing, always immaculate, looked strangely shabby on that day, and yet not one bit of it had changed. He wore the things he always wore.

The Earl's long black justacorps coat hung somewhat crumpled for its full length, right down to his mid-calf. The black velvet was curiously rumpled, and it caught Diana's eye and quietened her tears for a moment or two. His waistcoat and knee-breeches were also in a black velvet but looked less disarranged somehow. The frill at the neck of his white shirt was quite flattened, almost as if he had slept in the thing, and he carried a sturdy black tricorne hat under his arm and was wearing black, highly polished square-toed shoes with a gleaming rectangular buckle on the front. It was clear to all that Charles Spencer was leaving Althorpe for a while. He had somewhere to go, and he was going to leave his children to cry out their anguish without him.

"Where is Papa going?" Diana wailed into Anne's ear.

"I do not know, Di."

"But you could ask him."

"No, I could not."

"Then Robert can," Diana persisted. With one parent gone, never to return, her six-year-old self wanted to be absolutely sure of the whereabouts of her last remaining parent.

"We none of us may ask Papa. He is to be left alone at this time."

"But why?" Diana began to wail as she

watched the hunched figure of her father depart the room.

"It is just the way of things." Anne kissed the top of the little girl's head.

As Diana looked miserably about the drawing-room, she could see that both Charles and John were still crying, with their nurse and a maid doing their very best to provide comfort. Robert sat alone, trying for all the world to appear as if he had not shed a tear at all. He had rubbed hard at his cheeks and the skin around his eyes, but he had done so with grubby hands, and the dirty water stains on his face told their own story. Robert sat as still as a statue, averting his gaze from anyone who might try to console him. He seemed so terribly lonely and yet, at the same time, so very keen for solitude. He looked to Diana almost as her father had done as if he were simply a smaller version, and it made her love her eldest brother all the more.

"But what shall we do now, Anne?" Diana asked, feeling so small and afraid and wanting the reassurance of knowing that everybody around her knew what ought to be happening next.

"I really do not know," Anne said, trying hard to bite back her own sobs.

At that moment, the drawing-room door seemed almost to burst open and suddenly there appeared the Duke and Duchess of Marlborough. John Churchill, the Duke, stood silent in the centre of the room. His face looked grey and his eyes pained. He seemed quite as if he did not know what he should do next. The Duchess stood next to him, a woman who had already known the pain of the loss of a child, having already lost both a son and a daughter before either had reached their twentieth year. She had also lost two other children in infancy. Still, as she stood in the middle of the drawing-room, her face already beginning to crumble into a mask of grief, it was clear that she was suffering the sort of loss that no parent could ever grow used to.

"Grandmother!" Diana shouted and wriggled in Anne's arms, keen to be set free.

Diana wanted to run into the arms of another adult; a woman who would be able to sort everything out and tell them what they must do next. If anybody could help her, it was her grandmother.

Anne set her down and, as Diana raced across the room, her four siblings remained where they were. In truth, the Duchess of Marlborough was something of an acquired taste, even for her own children and grandchildren apparently. She had a harsh way of speaking and always spoke her mind. The Duchess did not like to be proved wrong and, if she had a point to make, she would continually make it until all around her acquiesced, commoners and royalty alike. However, to Diana, her grandmother represented safety and security. She represented the one adult amongst all adults who would always know what to do and when to do it. Grandmother would make everything all right again.

Even as a young girl, Diana had always wondered at her father's curious reaction to her mother's death. The Duchess of Marlborough had cried, and that was something that Diana could understand. A person in pain simply cried; that was how you knew that they were in pain.

However, not only had her father never shed a tear in her view but neither had he particularly spoken much of their mother again.

It had come as a great shock, therefore,

when just months later, the Earl of Spencer was ready to marry again.

"But who is this lady?" Diana, by then beginning to come to terms with the loss of her mother, stared up at her older sister incredulously.

"Her name is Judith Tichborne, Di, and she is a young lady from Ireland."

"But how does Papa come to know a lady from Ireland? How does Papa come to find another lady to marry?" Diana's young self felt a stab of outrage.

"I daresay in the same way that Papa married our own mother. He was married before then, you know. Papa's first wife died also," Anne said, a little sadly.

It was something that Diana had never really thought of before. Likely because she was simply a little girl to whom assorted relationships made little sense. Of course, she realised that she had an older sister, Frances, and she was vaguely aware that Frances and she did not share the same mother.

"The lady who was Frances' mother?" Diana looked up, her face a picture of confusion.

"Yes, Frances' mother was Lady Arabella Cavendish. That was the lady who was married to Papa before Mama. But she died, and so Papa married our mother. Do you understand now, Di?"

"Yes, I think so. I mean, I understand what happened, but I do not understand why. I mean, why does Papa need another wife now?"

"I suppose so that he will not be lonely. You would not wish Papa to be lonely, would you?"

"No, I would not," Diana said with all the conviction of a small child.

"And so, we will be able to welcome Judith Tichborne when she comes, will we not?" Anne said, rather hopefully.

"Yes, we shall," Diana said and nodded vigorously. "Is she just like Mama?"

"No, I do not think so." Anne faltered just a little. "You will probably find her rather more like me."

"Like you, Anne?"

"Yes. Judith Tichborne is the same age as me. Well, she is perhaps just a little older. But still, she is very young indeed."

"So why is Papa going to marry her?"

"Well, she is a very well-bred young lady from Ireland. And she has a very great fortune."

"Is she a lady like you, Anne?"

"She does not hold the title of *lady* as you and I do, but she comes from a very good family. Her father is a very successful man called Sir Benjamin Tichborne, and he is very keen that his daughter is married to Papa."

"That sounds nice," Diana said, thoughtfully. "But I do not think Grandmother will like it."

"I should imagine not, dear little Di, but Grandmother rarely likes anything, does she?" Anne said as she gave her little sister a mischievous smile.

Diana sank back into her pillows and sighed heavily as she thought back to that time. She could not think of her sadness at her mother's passing without crying, even nineteen years later. It always had the same effect upon her, and there seemed little she could do about it. Despite having been so very young when her mother passed, Diana had the very clearest impression of her in her mind. It was an impression that was so very different from every portrait that there was of Lady Anne Spencer. It was the very real impression that a child has of their mother. One of warmth, comfort, and security. One of love and forever and yet her portraits were so still, so formal.

As she looked back down the years, Diana realised that she had likely been so very accepting of the young Judith Tichborne simply because she was no more than a little girl who had yet to formulate such feelings as jealousy and spite.

In truth, Judith really was so very young that she could easily have been Diana's older sister in the way that Anne was. As she looked back, Diana realised that the young Irish woman was likely terrified of her new life and her new responsibilities. At just fifteen years of age, Judith was to be married to a man of one and forty years; easily old enough to be her own father. Of course, that was not uncommon by any means, and yet still Diana could not help but put herself in Judith's shoes and imagine quite how she might have felt at that age and in those circumstances.

When Judith Tichborne had arrived in Diana's life, it was not as a replacement for her mother or an adversary of any kind. Judith was simply a young woman in a new country and a new home that she had very likely had no choice about moving to. The new Countess of Sunderland was just a young woman who was as fearful and overawed as any other young woman in her position would likely have been.

Chapter Three

The coughing fit which seized Diana almost stopped her breathing altogether. She reached out for some water on the little table that her maid had placed at the side of her bed. However, her hand flailed wildly as she panicked and Diana simply knocked the glass from the table, sending it crashing to the ground with a piercing smash.

In no time at all, her maid arrived in the room, breathless and afraid.

"Oh, Your Grace! Your Grace!" she said, and her young eyes filled with tears.

Diana tried her very hardest to draw in the breath which seemed to be alluding her and, after a moment's fearful hesitation, her maid was at her side. She lifted Diana back into a sitting position.

"Stay calm, Your Grace," the maid said, trying to hide the fear in her own voice. "Now close your eyes for just a moment.

Diana did as the girl bid her, fearing there was nothing else left to do.

"Now slowly, so slowly, take a gentle breath. Nothing too big. Nothing that will set you off coughing again."

Diana stared into the darkness behind her eyes and wondered what it would feel like to simply give in to it. If she never took another breath, what would be waiting for her? Would she really see her Mama in Heaven, just the way Anne had told her that she would?

A feeling of the purest joy swept over

Diana, almost as if she truly had ascended into the Heavens. In truth, she could hardly remember having felt so very relaxed at any point in her life thus far. However, just as she felt herself truly prepared to let go of everything, Diana felt a slow and life-giving breath making its way into her nose and mouth and down into her cough-racked lungs.

"That's the way, Your Grace. That's the way," her maid said as she gently rubbed her mistress' back.

"Oh, thank you," Diana said, speaking gently so that she would not again antagonise her lungs.

Tasting the blood in her mouth, Diana looked up helplessly at the maid. Immediately gaining her mistress' meaning, the maid pulled a crisp white handkerchief from the pocket of her apron and handed it to her.

"Now, can you take a little water, Your

Grace?"

"I should very much like some water, but I am afraid that I broke the glass."

"I shall just go and collect you another, Your Grace. I shall be no more than one minute, I promise."

"How kind you are."

Diana's maid had returned in no time at all and, after drinking almost half a glass of water, Diana found herself feeling very much better. However, the fit of coughing had truly taken its toll upon her, and she was extremely tired.

"I think I shall take a little rest now," Diana said and smiled as the maid hurriedly rearranged her pillows and helped her to lay down.

"Would you like me to stay here with

you? I could sit in that chair by the window and watch over you for a while if it would make you feel any more relaxed, Your Grace."

"I should like that very much, my dear," Diana said gratefully.

"I shall stay quiet, Your Grace, whilst you take some sleep." And with that, the maid walked noiselessly across the room and sat in a small green velvet covered chair by the window, just as she had promised.

As Diana lay back on the sumptuous pillows, she looked up at the green velvet of the canopy above her. Once again, its colour put her in mind of health and well-being, of lush green meadows and leaves rustling on trees in the height of summer.

Once again, her thoughts drifted to the young Judith Tichborne, or Lady Judith Spencer as she had become. Diana remembered most clearly the swelling of the young woman's belly as, at the age of just sixteen years, Judith was expecting her first child.

The eight-year-old Diana had been inordinately excited at the prospect of a baby brother or sister of her very own. Up until that point, Diana had been the baby. She had been everybody's *dear little Di*, and she wanted someone even smaller upon whom she could lavish her own love and affection just as her brothers and sisters had done for her.

With sadness, Diana thought back to the day when Judith had lost the child she had been expecting. It was 1718, and the young Diana knew very little about babies, both their creation and how it was they came into the world. Hearing Judith cry all around the upstairs of Sunderland house, their London home in Piccadilly, Diana was at a loss to know what had happened. Judith's cries were truly heartbreaking, almost primal, and Diana knew that something dreadful must have happened. In the end, she sought out Anne. Anne would know what had happened; Anne would explain it all out to her.

"Anne, why does Judith cry so?" Diana asked when she came upon her sister in the library.

"Because she has lost her child, Di," Anne said, her countenance entirely sad.

"How can she have lost the child? The child has not been born yet." Diana was entirely confused.

"And the child will not be born now. At least not alive, my dear little Di."

"I do not understand, Anne."

"I know you do not, my dear, but then you are but eight-years-old. You should not have to understand such things."

"But you understand them."

"I understand them because I am myself sixteen years of age, the same age as Judith. I am old enough to bear a child myself, and so it is I understand exactly how one might be lost before it is even born. I shall simply say to you that something has happened inside Judith's body which has caused her tiny baby to die. I do not know how else to tell it to you, my dear little sister."

"You do not have to say anything else, Anne," Diana said, and she felt overwhelmed with sorrow, even though she did not understand exactly how any of it could be happening. "We shall just have to look after Judith until she feels better."

"You truly are the most wonderful and compassionate child," Anne said and scooped her younger sister into her arms. As she squeezed her tightly, a tear rolled down Anne's smooth, pale cheek. "And I do love you so, little one."

Sadly, for Lady Judith Spencer, this was not to be her first miscarriage. Just one year later, in 1719 when Diana was but nine-years-old, Judith once again miscarried a baby. With Anne's explanation, still fresh in her young mind, Diana did not have any questions to ask. Instead, she simply waited and watched and hoped for an opportunity to make Judith feel better.

When Judith conceived again, just twelve months later, the ten-year-old Diana hardly dared mention the pregnancy at all. In truth, none of them spoke much about it, almost as if to do so would somehow bring about yet another miscarriage. Judith, at only just eighteen years, walked quietly about the house as if a noise or sudden movement of any kind might change things for the worse.

Diana could see the pregnancy going

from strength to strength purely by studying the ever-growing belly of her father's wife. By the time Judith was in her eighth month, Diana had to fight every instinct in her body and instead hide the surge of excitement she felt. She was finally going to be a big sister, she felt sure of it.

The day that baby William made his way into the world, yelling and protesting all the way, was the happiest of Diana's young life. He was just so small and wrinkled and yet he was the most beautiful baby in all the world as far as Diana was concerned. She loved him immediately.

"When he gets a little bigger, Judith, would you let me hold him?" Diana had taken to following Judith and their nurse everywhere. She could not help but be amazed by the minute changes in William which seemed to take place every single day. It all seemed so very miraculous to her.

"You may hold him now if you wish." Judith smiled down indulgently at the little girl.

"Really? I should be so careful with him." Diana was excited enough to burst.

Diana sat in the deep red brocade covered armchair by the side of the fire in the baby's bed chamber. Gently, Judith placed the heavily wrapped bundle onto Diana's lap. He felt warm and surprisingly heavy for one born so small.

"He feels wonderful, Judith. He feels just like a little brother." Diana felt the tears of emotion, tears she could not yet explain, well up in her young eyes.

"And so he is, my dear little Di," Judith said, calling Diana by the pet name the rest of the family used for her.

The next two years were far happier for Diana than those preceding. She spent much of her time playing with her baby brother and watching as William grew into a more substantial infant. He was a bright and happy child who soaked up every moment of attention Diana lavished upon him.

As the Spring of 1722 awoke bringing with it the beautiful yellow of the daffodils and the exciting reds of the tulips, Diana's life seemed to be continuing without incident. William had a little ailment of some sort, but nothing out of the ordinary. He was quiet one moment and complaining the next, just like any baby with some childhood malady or other.

Diana began to wonder if her father shared William's malady, for he too looked less full-cheeked and his pallor had taken a distinct turn of greyness. Something about the Earl's looks reminded Diana painfully of six years prior when her own dear mother had died. The Earl had looked gaunt and grey then too.

As the days went on, William was quiet more often than he was complaining, and yet his health had not seemed to improve. Judith became more withdrawn which made Diana begin to fear that all was not well.

"Is William getting any better, Judith? He is very quiet." Diana followed Judith into William's chamber once more.

"He has a little fever, Di, but he ought to be getting over the worst of it by now." Judith smiled as she reached into the crib where baby William lay quietly sleeping.

Judith laid the back of her hand upon the infant's forehead, and suddenly her smile dropped, almost as if it had been erased from her face by an unseen hand.

"What is it?" Diana asked as her heart

began to thump. She knew something was wrong and, although she did not know what exactly, Diana felt suddenly sweaty and nauseous with fear.

"We need a physician. William is burning." Judith's eyes were wide with fear.

It had taken no time at all to have a physician sent to the house and, as he strode through the great entrance hall towards the stairs, he cast a look in the direction of the Earl.

"Perhaps when I have looked at the child, My Lord, it might be prudent for me to examine you also." The physician said, looking a little grave.

By the end of that day, baby William had gone. He had passed away as his mother sobbed at his bedside. Diana had never heard such expressions of grief in all her life as she had heard in the cries of Lady Judith Spencer.

It was the most heart-breaking noise that Diana had ever heard, even worse than the cries she had heard when Judith had lost her first baby.

Diana herself could not be consoled. At twelve years, she now fully understood death and how very final the whole thing was. No more did she think she would see the dearly departed again on this earth before the time came for Diana herself to ascend into Heaven, whenever that might be. She knew immediately that William would not be coming back.

Diana already missed baby William more than she could put into words. He had been so much of her day; so much of her young life had been spent in his amusement. On her second morning without sleep, as Diana walked into the drawing-room she saw Anne, now a woman of twenty years, standing before her, her face strewn with tears.

A feeling of the deepest fear seized

Diana when she looked up into her sister's face. This was something further; something more had happened.

Just two days after the heartbreak of the death of her baby brother, Diana's father, the Earl of Sunderland, had also died.

Chapter Four

1735

"Let me help you to sit back a little straighter against your pillows." The Dowager Duchess of Marlborough tried to hide her deep concern from her granddaughter.

Once again, Diana had been seized by a great fit of coughing. It was a particularly violent bout and Diana, already exhausted, was struggling to cover her mouth. As a consequence, fine droplets of blood dappled the crisp white linens covering her bed.

Prior to that afternoon, her

grandmother had only seen her coughing into handkerchiefs and had never witnessed anything quite so distressing. Diana could see the fear in her grandmother's eyes, and it was a terrible sight.

For as long as she could remember, her grandmother had been, quite simply, the strongest person in all the world. There was nothing that the Dowager Duchess of Marlborough could not achieve. If her grandmother looked afraid, then Diana felt sure there was a reason to be afraid.

"You should not be near me when I am coughing so, Grandmother," Diana said in between gasping breaths. "You know that the disease is more infectious when I am coughing."

"That is if you do, indeed, have tuberculosis, my dear girl," the Dowager Duchess said defiantly, although Diana felt sure she could see the resignation in her eyes. Finally, her dear grandmother was going to have to face the fact that her favourite granddaughter most certainly did have tuberculosis.

"Well, one thing I can tell you with surety, Grandmother, is that my symptoms are in no way a sign of pregnancy, are they?"

"But you did suffer the morning sickness, my dear."

"Indeed, I did, Grandmother, and I truly believe that I was, in the beginning at any rate, with child. However, it has become clear to me now that, at the very same time as I conceived, I also contracted this dreadful disease. Is that not simply the cruellest thing of all?"

"Are you sure that you did conceive, Di? After all, could not the vomiting have been part of whatever illness you now have? Is there really such a need to torture yourself in this manner?"

"Grandmother, I felt it," Diana said, tears rolling down her cheeks. "And I know I have felt it only twice before in my life. I was with child. I carried life within me at that moment."

"My dear little Di." Her grandmother sighed sadly.

"It is true, Grandmother. I felt it when I became pregnant with John, and I felt it again just months after he died when I had achieved my second pregnancy. This third pregnancy was even more short-lived, Grandmother, but I know that it was real. I know what I felt."

"And have you yet told John that you are no longer with child?"

"No, Grandmother, I have not. He has not been here to tell. He is, as I said in my letter, returned to Woburn Abbey with no hint as to when he might again come to Southampton House."

"But could you not write it to him? Would not a letter make things just a little easier for you?"

"Indeed, it would be so much easier, Grandmother. And yet I cannot do it. I must deliver the news in person, for one day I shall have to face it. I shall have to face his disappointment once again. Writing a letter to him will not spare me that. After all, he has spent these last two years blaming me for the loss of my last child."

"It makes me despise him, Di." The Dowager Duchess was suddenly vehement.

"In truth, sometimes it makes me despise him also." Diana sighed and closed her eyes as she leant back heavily into the immense white pillows. "Especially when I realise that he also blamed me for John's death."

"For Heaven's sake, Di, that was an accident. How on earth could you have prevented it?"

"According to John, by never setting foot in a carriage in the first place. By never making any journey of any kind whilst I was so heavily with child. He has said it so many times over that I have come to believe it is true. If I had simply stayed in the house on that day, then my first child would still be alive, would he not?"

"But you cannot look at it in that manner, Diana. You cannot look back at life and ask *what if I did this?* and *what if I did not do that?* You simply live life, my dear, and accept whatever comes your way."

"But if I had stayed in the house on that day, my first child would still be alive."

"Maybe, he would… but maybe the Lord had plans for him and would simply have used some other method. If those were the rules by which you choose to live, you would never move from the spot you stand upon. You would never dare take a step and, slowly but surely, you would wither and die. That is not how life is meant to be lived, my dear little Di."

"You are so very strong, Grandmother, and I wish myself as determined as you." Diana looked vaguely down at the blood splattered linens and wished that her grandmother did not have to contemplate such a thing.

For a moment, Diana considered calling in the maid and asking her to change the linens for her. However, she knew well that the act would interrupt her meeting with her grandmother and Diana could not have borne it. She needed the Dowager Duchess more than she had ever needed another person in her life. She always had.

"Yes, I am strong, Diana. But the blood which runs through my veins also runs through yours. I come from the Jenyns, and we Jenyns are hardy folk. And you have your grandfather's Churchill blood too. You have the best of both worlds, Di, if only you could know it. You are strong by birth, and you have more sense than any woman I know."

"Oh, Grandmother! You have said that to me before. And you have said it to others too, I have heard you." Diana laughed weakly.

"I have said it so often because it is true. You have made me prouder than any other person in this world has done and I want only the very best for you."

"I know you do, Grandmother, you always have."

"I remember the day you first came to me, my sweet child," The Dowager Duchess said wistfully.

"It was such a difficult time, Grandmother. We seemed to be losing everything we had. Everyone who was important to us and everyone we loved."

"Yes, and you managed it all with dignity and grace, my child. There cannot be another one of just twelve years who has managed things the way you did."

Shortly after her father's death, Diana was adopted by her maternal grandmother. With her siblings, all older than she and none of them having the same depth of feeling for their grandmother that Diana did, she went alone. Diana had always been the Duchess of Marlborough's favourite.

Diana had always loved Marlborough House, where her grandmother lived, almost as much as her grandmother herself did. There was just something about it that was so much warmer and more inviting than Blenheim Palace. And Blenheim was not truly finished, even then. The Dowager Duchess still enjoyed many an argument with the architect over this and that and, although she had devoted many years to overseeing the building of what should have been her husband's principal residence, still she referred to it deprecatingly as *that pile of stones*. Secretly, the expression had always made Diana laugh, as had the idea of her ageing grandparent arguing volubly with the men who had devoted their lives to the understanding of great building works and architectural wonders.

It had not been until 1719 that the Duke and Duchess of Marlborough had been able to move into the finished east wing of the palace.

As much as Diana adored Oxfordshire and loved to run and play in the beautiful grounds of Blenheim, still, she always associated Marlborough House in Pall Mall with her grandparents, more particularly her grandmother.

Diana's grandfather, John Churchill, had suffered greatly in his health over the last years. Little more than a month after the death of his daughter, Lady Anne Spencer, when he had stood bereft in the drawing-room of Diana's home, the Duke of Marlborough suffered a terrible stroke. The stroke left him paralysed for a time, although he had begun to regain some mobility. However, in November of 1716, he suffered a further stroke which affected his speech greatly.

But, with the loving care of his faithful and tenacious wife, the Duke had recovered enough to be able to occasionally ride over to Blenheim where he watched the workmen as they continued to build his great country home and he was still able to attend the House of Lords on occasion when he needed to vote.

Before Diana had been born, her grandfather was the First Lord of the Treasury for eight years, and her grandmother spoke of it often in the years she and Diana lived together. The Dowager Duchess had been keen that Diana should know well her family's history and be as proud of the old Duke of Marlborough as his wife had always been.

Despite being in full control of his wits, John Churchill never fully mastered his speech ever again. Just months after baby William and Diana's father, the Earl of Sunderland, had died, her beloved grandfather, the Duke of Marlborough, died also.

"Why does everybody have to die, Grandmother?" Diana, just twelve-years-old, had asked the Dowager Duchess through a mouthful of bread and butter as they took afternoon tea in the drawing room of Marlborough house.

"Well, we all have to die in the end, my dear. That is the only way that we can get to Heaven." Diana could tell that her grandmother had not slept properly for many days.

John Churchill had been the great love of Sarah Jenyn's life, and his loss was weighing very heavily upon her. It gave young Diana almost physical pain to see her grandmother so sad.

"But why do some go to Heaven sooner than others? Why did my Mama die when she was still so young? And why did baby William die too? Surely, he was not here on earth long enough to go back into Heaven. He was but two-years-old."

"I cannot answer those questions for you, my dear little Di. I wish I could. But we none of us know the answers to all of it, and can only manage what is here before us on this earthly plain and in this moment."

"Will I die young because my mama did?" Diana asked with a child's logic.

"No, my dear. I am two and sixty years myself and yet my own dear Anne, your mother, died at only three and thirty. There is no way of knowing what will become of us and when we shall depart this earthly life."

"There are no rules to it, are there?"

"None, my dear child. That is why we must make the most of the life we are given. We must seize every opportunity which comes our way in this world."

"But what happens if opportunities do not come our way? How shall we seize them then?" Diana looked at her grandmother wide-eyed. The Dowager Duchess always knew what to do and what to say.

"Then we make our own opportunities.

We turn every circumstance to its best light possible and make an opportunity out of it."

"Is that what I ought to do, Grandmother?"

"Yes, Diana, it is." Her grandmother smiled warmly at her.

"But I do not know how."

"You do not need to worry, my dear little Di. I shall make your opportunities for you. You are my life now, my sweet child, and I have nothing but your health and happiness to attend to. You shall have every opportunity in this world, and I shall see to it myself."

Diana laughed at the memory and opened her eyes.

"Were you dreaming, my dear?" Her grandmother had not moved from her place by her side.

"Not dreaming, Grandmother, reminiscing."

"I am not sure reminiscence is a health-giving past-time." The Dowager smiled.

"In this case, I think it was. I was thinking of you and how you looked after me so well after Papa died. I was thinking about the day you taught me about seizing opportunities in life."

"Good. Then you shall remember it all very well when you are once again healthy. Then you shall be bright and ready to seize opportunities once again, and I shall be there, as always, to help you seize them."

Chapter Five

Diana awoke expecting to see her grandmother still at her bedside. When that good woman did not come into view, she slowly remembered saying goodbye to her. The Dowager Duchess had kissed her forehead and sworn to return the following day. But, despite the knowledge that her grandmother would certainly do as she had promised, still, Diana could find no peace. She wanted her back again if only to look into her beautiful soft and lined face, with the keen eyes which spoke of the sharp intellect dancing behind them.

Diana had always seen something in her grandmother that others saw in an entirely different way. Where others saw a pushy nature and raw, untamed ambition, Diana saw a strength of will and the determination to make a difference in her own lifetime. Curiously, men who pursued the same undertaking were applauded everywhere they went. They were men of character, men of Parliament, men of action. Women were not so applauded for it. And yet the men of action who had surrounded Sarah Churchill throughout her life had all made some, if not all, of their achievements with her help.

When Diana first moved to live with her grandmother, she had delighted in the stories of the days before she herself was born. At those times her grandmother had been one of the biggest political influences in the country.

"I was a great friend to Queen Anne, you know," The Dowager Duchess had told the young Diana, and not for the first time.

Diana smiled, the tales never bored her, and she knew that if she herself went on to achieve but *half* the wonders her grandmother had done, then she too would think they bore repeating.

"Even before she was Queen?" The sixteen-year-old Diana knew how to play her part well.

"Yes, indeed. When her father, James II, was deposed by Prince William of Orange and his wife, James' own daughter, Mary, I stood by her. I even helped her to escape to the north country when her father placed us both under house arrest."

"And you did whatever you could to further her cause when you worked for the Royal household of King William and Queen Mary," Diana supplied helpfully.

"I most certainly did. King William was easier to deal with than Queen Mary. Although Anne's sister, Mary, wanted nothing more than to split the two of us apart. She even demanded that Anne dismiss me. Anne refused, of course, and Mary never forgave her for it."

"But then Queen Mary died."

"Yes, and King William followed her eight years later. It was 1702, and Anne was finally the Queen."

"And you continued to stand by her side." Diana smiled warmly. She knew the story had a less than warm ending, but still, she wanted nothing more than to humour her grandmother through the telling of the happier times.

"I did," the Dowager said, a little sadly. "And there were many who came to me because they knew I had the ear of the Queen. There were never two closer friends than we. Well, at that time, anyway."

"Even the politicians came to you,

Grandmother," Diana said, brightly.

"Indeed, they did. Your grandfather and dear Lord Godolphin went to the very top of government. Your grandfather's appointment as First Lord of the Treasury in 1702 was entirely due to my own efforts with Queen Anne. Still, they both knew it well and never once did they forget it. When your grandfather was away, Lord Godolphin always turned to me for political advice."

Diana stifled a laugh; over the years she had heard the account told a little differently. Whilst she knew Sidney Godolphin and her grandmother to have been the closest of friends, she also knew that Sarah Churchill's outspokenness, bossiness, and determination to have her way in all things had driven poor Lord Godolphin to distraction. Furthermore, that same tenacity of nature had finally worn down her grandmother's relationship with Queen Anne.

"They both appreciated your skill in politics, Grandmother."

"They did. And Queen Anne used to value my advice most highly. Still, Abigail Masham had put an end to all of that," The Dowager said, bitterly.

Diana knew more of the truth of it since, once in a moment of weakness, her grandmother had confessed her own part in the breakdown of her relationship with the Queen. She had told Diana that she had perhaps pushed the Queen a little too far to openly support the Whigs and had argued with her most bitterly on the way to a Thanksgiving service at St Paul's Cathedral. Sarah had insisted that the Queen openly support the Whigs. When Queen Anne had continued to argue her own point in the cathedral itself, the Duchess of Marlborough told her to be quiet. She had silenced the Queen! It saw the start of the true unravelling of their long friendship, and Sarah Churchill bitterly regretted it. She even apologised for her behaviour, something that the Duchess rarely did. Unfortunately, it was too late.

"She had become close to the Queen," Diana said, quietly. In truth, she wished her grandmother would not go on with the tale, but simply leave it to stand still where it was.

"My own cousin. When I think how it was I who raised her up out of poverty and introduced her at Court. Without my considerable influence, Abigail would never have become the Lady of the Bedchamber to the Queen... if I had not worked upon it all in her favour."

"She worked her way into the Queen's affections," Diana said exactly what she knew her grandmother wanted to hear.

The truth was that Abigail Masham had

been a kinder and gentler confidante than the Duchess of Marlborough and was able to show compassion to the Queen when she felt unwell. Furthermore, she did not care at all about politics, so she did never try to influence the Queen. As the Queen's health failed, she no doubt found Abigail's friendship so much easier to maintain. Sarah, on the other hand, was simply too argumentative and energetic for a person with failing health to deal with.

"Still, the Queen did not make our separation public for many years. She quite rightly did not want anything to undermine your grandfather's role as Captain-General of the Army. She needed him too much, you see."

Diana knew that to be true, for she had heard it from many lips. However, when her grandparents had involved parliament in a failed attempt to force Anne to dismiss Abigail Masham, Queen Anne decided she no longer needed the Duke of Marlborough and fashioned some kind of spurious embezzlement charge as a means of dismissing him.

"I shall never forget the day I had to return my golden key. It was one of the most painful experiences of my life."

Diana knew, of course, that her grandmother had finally been dismissed from Queen Anne's household and had returned the gold key which had been a symbol of her authority there.

It had not been until Queen Anne had died in 1714 and the Hanoverians had taken the throne that she and her husband were once more in Royal favour.

Although her grandmother rarely acknowledged her part in the loss of her friendship with Queen Anne, Diana knew in her heart that it was a source of great regret and sadness to her. Sometimes she wished she could have been there and could have helped and yet she knew it was not possible.

As the years went on and Diana grew into womanhood, she and her grandmother became inseparable.

The Dowager Duchess frequently suffered from attacks of gout and often found it difficult to write. As such, Diana became her grandmother's full-time personal assistant from a young age and would read and answer many letters at the Dowager's behest.

As Diana grew up, she blossomed into a strikingly beautiful young woman. With her grandmother being one of the richest women in Europe, Diana's beauty and connection to the Dowager Duchess made her one of the most sought after young ladies in the country. Furthermore, despite her grandmother's often terse nature, Diana herself was a charming and mild-mannered young woman whose compassion knew no bounds. She was as kind and caring as she was beautiful, and she turned heads wherever she went.

"You have grown up, my dear little Di. Whatever shall I do when you are married away with a life and a family of your own?" Her grandmother teased as the two prepared themselves for one in an endless line of evening engagements.

"You know we shall never be truly parted, Grandmother. I could not hear of it, nor could I manage without you." Diana, whilst speaking to soothe, truly meant what she said. She adored the Dowager Duchess more than she could say.

"But you must marry one day, my dear. I cannot keep you forever."

"I am not yet twenty, Grandmother. There is time enough for me to marry." Diana really meant it.

She had never regretted for a moment that she had been adopted and raised by her grandmother. The Dowager Duchess was the very cornerstone of Diana's young life and had always symbolised safety and security. Despite the fact that she knew it would have to happen eventually... she was not entirely keen to relinquish the comfort which such assurances provided. Marriage was a very different life and one which held no such certainties.

If only she could be married away to a man like her grandfather. One who would cherish her and listen to her own little opinions on things, just as her grandfather had done with her grandmother. Still, men of that nature were few and far between, and Diana knew that as well educated and wise as she knew herself to be, she did not have the tenacity of spirit that her grandmother possessed. Sarah Churchill had played politics as a woman in a world of men and had cared not one bit about it. She had shrugged off the opinions of all and followed her own path without apology. Diana feared that she could never be the same herself, and knew that wishing would not make it so.

"And yet there is no time like the present." Her grandmother laughed mischievously.

"What do you mean? You have not already found a husband for me and said nothing of it, surely?" Diana's heart began to beat as furiously as a racing horse as she felt herself suddenly a little afraid.

Now it seemed entirely likely that her grandmother had engineered this conversation and, as always, Diana had not realised until it was too late.

"No, I have not done such a thing, my dear little Di. But still, I shall start looking soon. I cannot leave such a thing to chance."

"But *why* can you not simply leave it to chance?" Diana said, relieved and a little amused. Her grandmother approached everything in the same way; politics, house building, and the arranging of marriages for her children and grandchildren.

"Because *chance* gives no assurances of achieving the very best, my dear. Chance is just that; chance! It can work well, or it can go most disastrously. That is the whole point of chance, and that is why I choose never to entertain it as a concept."

"Goodness me," Diana said and laughed heartily. "I rather fear for myself in this match-making scheme of yours. In truth, I rather fear for the eligible bachelors of England if this is your approach."

"You may laugh at your grandmother, child, but you know well that I shall see you married to nothing but the very best of men."

"I can hardly think that there is any such man in the country who would suit you. You take too great a care of me to ever think any man is good enough." Diana continued to tease.

"Whilst that is true I still have hopes of securing the very best for you."

"And what sort of man do you deem to be the very best, Grandmother?" As she said the words, she thought of a handsome prince, who was sweet and kind, just like her grandfather.

It took but a second for her grandmother to answer. "I shall find you a prince, my dear little Di."

Chapter Six

As Diana lay in her chamber in the Southampton house, she thought longingly of the chamber that had been hers for many years. The one in her grandmother's favourite home, Marlborough House.

The great bed hangings there had been a deep russet-coloured brocade, and whenever she had closed them, she had felt herself protected from the world. Nothing existed beyond her large bed; nothing outside the great brocade drapes existed.

Dreamily, she thought of her bed linens and the warm, russet-coloured bedspread which protected her linens and kept them spotlessly white. Throughout her room, the great oak panelling on the walls had been a pale fawn colour. It had been a wonderful contrast to the russet and made her drapes and bedspread look ever richer. It had been the place of her late childhood, the place where she had felt absolute safety in the love and protection of her grandmother. It had been her home, and she missed it dearly.

"Good afternoon, my dear. I have been here a little while, but your maid told me you were sleeping so peacefully."

Diana thought it very apt that, at the moment she was thinking of the security of her childhood, the very woman who had brought such a feeling about appeared suddenly in her chamber at Southampton House.

"Indeed, Grandmother, I have just now this minute awoken."

"I have asked the maid to bring a little food for you, my dear."

"But Grandmother, I am not hungry," Diana said weakly. In fact, the thought of food turned her stomach.

"Whether you are hungry or not, child, you must eat. You are wasting away before my eyes."

Diana felt tears prick at the back of her eyes. She fought them down but could not stop the words that seemed to come with a will of their own. "I am being consumed by the tuberculosis, Grandmother. No amount of food will put that to rights."

"Diana, I shall not have this. I shall not stand and see you give in to this thing. You are to fight it, my dear, and you must start first by eating."

"Then I shall do as you ask," Diana said,

wondering how she would even find the energy to chew.

"It is nothing more than a little cold meat and some red wine. Still, it shall do more good in your belly than it shall by wasting on the plate." The Dowager Duchess smiled. "Ah, here comes the maid now."

The Dowager Duchess opened the door allowing the young maid to bustle through with the tray of assorted meats and an enormous glass of red wine. She laid the tray down on the table and made as if she would assist the Duchess of Bedford to eat.

"You may leave us, my dear," Diana's grandmother said politely. "I shall help my granddaughter to eat."

"Very well, Your Grace," the young maid said quietly before curtsying deeply and leaving the room.

"It does look like an awful lot of meat," Diana said plaintively. "I shall do my very best, but I very much doubt I shall be able to manage it all."

"Then I shall help you to manage as much as you can, my dear. Now, let me help you sit up a little straighter."

With the most tender loving care, Diana's grandmother, at five and seventy years of age, helped her granddaughter to move back in the bed far enough to lean herself against the great pile of pillows she had arranged.

Lifting the tray and placing it on the bed beside Diana, the Dowager Duchess perched on the bed behind it and began to cut the meat into small squares, so tiny that her granddaughter would barely have to chew them.

"Now eat, my dear little Di."

Diana ate as much of the meat as she could possibly manage and drank all of the wine at her grandmother's behest.

"You have done very well indeed."

"Thank you, Grandmother. In truth, I do feel a little better."

"It has restored your colour just a little, my dear. But do you not see? This is the way that we shall make you well again. And you shall be well again, Diana. Please believe me when I tell you that you shall, for I know it to be true."

"Indeed, I believe I shall need all of my strength in the coming days."

"For what purpose?"

"I have received a letter from John," Diana said and winced a little. "It was rather brief, simply informing me of his intention to attend Southampton House at the end of the week. Of course, he still has pressing matters to attend to at Woburn Abbey, so he shall not be able to stay for long."

"And did you return his letter?"

"Only to acknowledge the receipt of his. I said nothing else."

"Then he still does not know."

"He still does not know." Diana looked downcast, and the colour began to drain from her face once more.

"Well, I am sure that you shall manage that day as well as you have managed all the difficulties in your life. You have the strength to get through it, Diana. I know that you do."

"Thank you."

"In the meantime, however, let us talk of other things; lighter things. I have no desire to build you up with food and bring you down with the wrong conversation."

"I thank you. What should we talk about?" Diana brightened just a little.

"Tell me, have you had any more of your happy reminiscences since last I saw you?"

"Indeed, I have." Diana laughed but stopped abruptly as a cough welled in her chest.

She coughed lightly and was relieved to find there was no blood and that the coughing subsided almost as quickly as it had begun.

"And what have you been thinking of?" The Dowager spoke as if to ignore the small coughing fit entirely; as if to deny the existence of the tuberculosis would be to successfully banish it somehow.

"I was thinking of your determined

efforts to find me a suitable husband."

"Perhaps that was not as successful a mission as I had first hoped it would be."

"Indeed not, but it was done with love as always, and I cannot help but remember that time and your efforts so very fondly."

"Then you do me a great kindness, Di." The Dowager smiled.

"Do you remember the letter from the dear Earl of Chesterfield?" Diana asked with a sweet smile of her own.

"Indeed, I do." The Dowager winced. "The poor man."

The Dowager Duchess' efforts to find the perfect match for her granddaughter had been matched almost entirely by the efforts of so many men, both young and not-so-young, who thought to seek Diana's hand unbidden.

Diana could hardly believe that it was only four years before that life had seemed to be so very full of hope. In truth, she had found herself entirely caught up in her grandmother's search for the very best of husbands. It had been a thrilling and exciting time, and she could not help but look back on it with longing. If only!

Diana had grown into such a beauty that her confidence had ridden at an all-time high and she almost took for granted how many young men seemed to want her attention.

One such potential suitor had been Thomas Thynne, the Viscount of Weymouth. He was the grandson of the Duke of Somerset and had inherited the beautiful Longleat Estate when he was but four-years-old. Diana had always thought him rather a handsome young man and had always felt a little for the losses he had suffered.

The Viscount of Weymouth's own father had died four months before he had been born and something about that rather stimulated Diana's sympathy. As early on as she had lost her own parents, at least she had known them and could draw them to mind without the need of referring to inaccurate portraits. As far as she was concerned, poor Thomas Thynne could do no such thing and she thought it a terrible pity.

Born in 1710, Thomas Thynne was the very age that Diana herself was. And like Diana, Thomas had gone on to suffer yet more losses and yet more grief. At the age of just sixteen, Thomas had married Lady Elizabeth Sackville, only to suffer her death just three years later in 1729. A widower at just nineteen years, the Viscount and his deceased wife had had no children. As he approached his twenty-first year, Thomas had made it known that he was keen to secure the hand of Lady Diana Spencer.

However, the Dowager Duchess of Marlborough would hear nothing of it. She had no particular animosity towards the young man himself, rather she simply thought that he was not quite good enough. The Dowager wanted more for her granddaughter than a mere viscount.

Shortly thereafter, Anthony Ashley-Cooper, the Earl of Shaftesbury, also began to make his feelings known. Again, he was a man of Diana's own age, born just one year after she herself. Diana found him also rather handsome, not to mention well-read and rather scholarly. And yet still, he was not good enough in the eyes of the Dowager Duchess of Marlborough.

Finally, in August of 1731, the Dowager Duchess herself received a letter from yet another man who saw himself a potential suitor for the young and beautiful Lady Diana

Spencer. The man himself was Philip Stanhope, the Earl of Chesterfield. He was not only charmed by the young Diana but also a great friend of her grandmother.

"Dear me, I have a letter here from dear Philip Stanhope," the Dowager said as she leafed through the correspondence that Diana had dutifully opened for her and laid out on a tray.

"Oh, I do hope he is well, Grandmother. Does he say how his trip to the Netherlands proceeds?" Diana had always rather liked the Earl of Chesterfield. He was, at that time, more than seven and thirty years of age. He was a terribly learned man and a great speaker, always coming up with such quotes as to delight the listener entirely. On many an occasion, Diana had enjoyed the older man's company greatly, finding herself always pleased to discover she was at an event at which he himself attended.

"He does not talk of the Netherlands, my dear."

"He mentions nothing of his trip at all?" Diana ceased in opening the rest of the letters for her grandmother and stared across at her incredulously. "But surely he says something of it."

"He does not speak of it, my dear, not at all."

"Then what does he speak of, Grandmother?"

"He speaks of you, predominantly," the Dowager Duchess said with a sigh.

"He speaks of me?"

"Perhaps it would be easier if I simply read an excerpt to you."

"Please do."

"He writes, *the person, the merit and the family of Lady Diana Spencer are objects so valuable that they must necessarily have....caused many such applications of this nature to Your Grace.*"

"What applications, Grandmother? Of what nature?" Diana said, her heart sinking.

In truth, she knew exactly what the short passage had meant, and how she wished she did not. How well she liked the older man and how much unease of heart it would give her to think him in any way downcast by her rejection.

"You shall have to write back to him, my dear."

"But, Grandmother! Whatever shall I say?"

"You shall not be saying it, my dear little Di. Have no fear that you are breaking his heart, for it shall be *I* who takes that responsibility."

"I am to write in your name?"

"As you always do, my dear, when the gout is upon me. I shall dictate it to you, and you will simply write it for me. And you will sign my name, and not your own."

"That is very kind of you, Grandmother. After all, I know what great friends you are, and I know what pain it shall give you to feel that you are hurting him."

"Indeed, it shall," her grandmother said with a sigh.

"But he is too old for me, Grandmother, is he not?" Diana said, in an attempt to soothe her grandmother's emotions.

"Not only is he too old for you, my dear, but dear Philip Stanhope is not at all the man I have in mind to be your husband, and therefore I must tell him so."

"Does this mean that you *do* have a man in mind to be my husband, Grandmother?"

"Indeed, I do, child."

"And might I ask, my dear Grandmother, who that man might be?" Diana said and felt her mouth go a little dry as her heart began to jitter in her chest.

This was the moment she had been awaiting for some months. Diana had always known that her grandmother would come to a conclusion on the matter and that one day she would present it to her.

"The Prince of Wales, my dear."

Chapter Seven

As Diana spent a happy afternoon in reminiscence with her ageing grandmother, she stopped short of speaking about the Prince of Wales. Diana simply drew the conversation to a gentle conclusion at the receipt of the letter from the Earl of Chesterfield.

The plot her grandmother had contrived to see her granddaughter married into the Royal household of the Hanoverians had not gone well, and it was not a failure that Diana had any wish to remind her grandmother of. Even four years later, Diana herself still wished that her grandmother had never attempted such a thing. Whilst it had not done them any great detriment as a family, still it had been a most worrying time full of too much uncomfortable excitement which ended only in dashed hopes.

When her grandmother had casually announced that she fully intended Diana to marry the Prince of Wales, Diana had been unable to speak for several minutes.

"The Prince of Wales?" she squeaked when finally, her voice returned to her.

"Yes, my dear little Di, the Prince of Wales." The Dowager Duchess spoke so matter-of-factly that, at that moment, Diana could have almost believed it to be true.

"But how is such a thing to be managed, Grandmother? It cannot be true."

"Do not worry. I have my methods, and I am not afraid to use them. Who else would be good enough?"

Diana ignored most of that last part.

"Pray tell me, what are your methods in this instance, Grandmother? I beg that you would enlighten me."

"I have already been in some small conference with the Prince of Wales and very quickly discovered that he has great debts in his own right."

"I am not surprised, Grandmother. For it is told that he leads such a degenerate life!"

"Indeed, he does." The Dowager nodded significantly. "Which is why I have made it known that I have one-hundred-thousand pounds to give him as a settlement upon your marriage."

"One-hundred-thousand pounds, Grandmother!?" Diana said, her eyes as wide and as round as the moon.

"It is a sum that I think is worthy of such a union. He is next in the line of succession to the throne when his father, George II, dies."

"But what does his father say of the thing? What does the King himself think of such a proposal?"

"I do not yet know what the king thinks of it, my dear."

"You do not yet know? But I do not understand," Diana said her heart was pounding, and she felt a little lightheaded. "For a man... prince, to have such debts, surely that cannot be a good thing?"

"He is to be king one day, my dear. That is all you need to focus your attention upon. You need not think too deeply of his financial circumstances now, for they shall greatly improve when one day he is crowned."

"But what of his character, Grandmother?"

Diana had heard, as had most, the great gossip and stories which surrounded the young Prince of Wales. When he was just seven-years-old, his parents left him in the care of other family members in Hanover, Germany. Whilst they made their way to England at the behest of the newly crowned George I who had taken the throne upon the death of Queen Anne. The child did not see his parents again until the crowning of his own father, George II, in 1728. By then he was a fully-grown man of one and twenty years whose morals and behaviour, it was reported, had suffered greatly from the parental estrangement.

"A man's character can always be moulded by a strong wife, my dear."

"But a character such as his, Grandmother? There are tales of drinking and gambling which no doubt account for such great debts. More disturbingly, there is great talk of the women he associates with and the other company he keeps."

It was true that the resentful young Frederick seemed to battle against every opinion of his parents. Even as a music lover, he had favoured the Opera of the Nobility rather than the Opera of the King's Theatre, which had Royal approval and was favoured by his father. It was said that his degenerate behaviour was intended more as an antagonism towards his parents than as a true delight of his own. But still, his behaviour did not give her confidence that he would be the husband she could love. That he could be a man to share and partner with in the way her grandmother and grandfather had. It did not lead her to believe he could make her happy and for a moment she was filled with melancholy.

"Do not fear, he is a young man and, as yet, has no matrimonial tie. Of course, he seeks the company of a certain type of woman. But that will stop when he is married to a beauty such as you, Di."

"Grandmother, I shrink to tell you this, but I have heard it said that the Prince of Wales shares a mistress with Baron Hervey of Ickworth. Her name is Anne Vane, and she is the wayward daughter of Baron Barnard. She has had several affairs and does nothing to hide it." Diana could not hide her feeling, even though she tried.

"Yes, I have heard it. And I have no doubt of it. After all, John Hervey and the Prince are great friends."

"So great that they share a mistress!" Diana felt rather scandalised by it all.

"My dear, they are young men out and about in a world of privilege. That sort of thing changes when they fall in love. And fall in love with you he shall, my dear, for do not all men fall in love with you?"

"Does it really change, Grandmother?"

"Yes, and not only is it a simple hurdle to overcome, my dear, but it is only his raucous behaviour which provides us with this particular opportunity. And do you remember, my dear girl, what I told you about opportunities?"

"That they must be seized as they present themselves, Grandmother," Diana said quietly.

"Indeed, they must." The Dowager Duchess reached out and took her granddaughter's hands. "And I should not let you go to anyone less. His degenerate ways will stop, my dear, I have no doubt of it. But I can only secure such a great match for you because the man himself is in debt. But everything else that you wish for shall follow thereafter. He will fall in love with you and one day you shall be his Queen."

"Have you really had some conference with him, Grandmother?"

"Indeed, I have, my dear."

"And do you really think that he will be favourable to such a proposal?"

"A beautiful and well-bred lady with a grandmother of such a large fortune is irresistible to any man, prince and pauper alike."

"Even one who has scars, Grandmother? After all, I am not the great beauty I once was, am I?"

"My dear girl, the surgeon has done such wonderful work to restore you, and you are as beautiful now as you have always been. I shall not hear you say otherwise, Diana, for I know your beauty to be clear to all who lay eyes upon you."

In truth, Diana really was still very beautiful indeed. However, just a year before, she had suffered a most dreadfully disfiguring skin condition. The physicians had called it tuberculosis cervical lymphadenitis, although it was more commonly known as scrofula. It had been caused by some manner of infection in the lymph nodes, and its effects had been devastating upon the young Diana.

A great mass had developed on her neck and had continued to grow and grow, finally tearing at the skin and turning it a dreadful bluish purple colour.

Diana had felt herself most terribly disfigured and had refused to go out anywhere, keeping to Marlborough House for the entire time she suffered the dreadful thing. In the end, the Dowager Duchess of Marlborough had employed one of the finest surgeons that money could buy. It was he who had excised the thing and had done his very best to keep the scarring that ensued light and unobtrusive.

When first she had begun to heal, Diana had used a patch box, much as those who had suffered smallpox tended to use. It was a little box which contained small pieces of taffeta or even silk, and one could apply them on the skin with an adhesive of sorts, in an attempt to disguise pock-marks. In truth, Diana had found them of little use on her own scarring, and in the end resorted to the heavy use of lead face powder. The face powder had whitened her skin beautifully and hidden the scarring very well indeed.

However, Diana had always, from then onwards, been most conscious of the scarring, regardless of how well she could hide it.

Of course, keeping her fair hair long and having much of it loose whenever her hair was strongly curled using hot tongs, did much to keep her neck from view.

But was that enough to please a prince? Was that enough to ensure he thought her pretty in all ways; pretty enough to be a princess and to one day be his Queen?

"But he is a prince, Grandmother," Diana said, sadly. "Will he not look for perfection in his princess?"

"Initially, my dear girl, he is simply looking for money."

"I can hardly explain how that makes me feel." Diana had felt herself a little silent, wishing that her grandmother would not continue to talk about any future marriage of hers as a simple business arrangement. "I had always thought that you wanted the best for me, Grandmother."

"And the best is what I shall find you,

my dear. The best that I can possibly do for you is to marry you into the Royal household, can you not see that? Can you not see what great sacrifices I make to ensure that the very best opportunities come your way?"

"Of course, I can, Grandmother. Forgive me, but I cannot help but be concerned. It is the dream of every young lady to become a princess, of that I have no doubt. In truth, it has always been a silly dream of my own. But perhaps the reality of it will be so very different from the dream."

"I feel sure that it will be a success, my darling."

"But, Grandmother, what if his character does not change? What if he continues along the path he has always walked, intent only upon the money you are offering him?" Diana looked down towards the floor. "What if he continues to share a mistress with Lord Hervey?"

"My dear child, there are never any guarantees in a marriage. Men are what they are, and it is for us women to make the best of it. I want a marriage that secures you the very best position in life and everything you could ever want.

I want you to have influence as I never quite had, and I want you to use it in the very best way. Imagine the good you could do if you were a princess, or better yet, Frederick's Queen when finally he takes the throne.

You would have the ear of the most powerful man in all the country. Even I, with all my plots and schemes and hard work never quite managed that. Yes, I often had the ear of Queen Anne when she was on the throne, but not always did she agree with me. And the ear of a husband, especially one who dotes upon his wife, is of value without measure.

You could have the life that I have had,

only better. You can have your opinions heard and work hard on behalf of the Whigs. Imagine the influence you would have, and imagine the good you would do. A mistress or two along the way will be no hardship when you have so many other privileges to be glad for.

Sarah J Freeman

.

Chapter Eight

When finally she was alone again, Diana thought back to the days of worry she had hidden so successfully from her grandmother. In the end, she had simply acquiesced, knowing that her grandmother was too formidable an opponent to fight. What was worse, Diana loved the Dowager Duchess more than life itself and would have done nothing in the world to go against her.

If her life was to be with Frederick, Prince of Wales, then she would choose to accept it.

Diana tried to sit up a little straighter in bed with the idea of levering herself up and perhaps taking a few steps about her bedchamber. Something about her reminiscences was making her feel somehow that she was betraying her grandmother with her own memories. Diana wanted to rise to her feet and walk the feeling away; she wanted to settle the whole thing in her mind and forget it forever.

However, she found that she barely had the strength to pull the great pile of linens and the thick bedspread from over her legs. By the time she had freed herself from her many coverings, she was utterly exhausted. Without even the strength to pull the covers back up over herself, Diana simply flopped backwards, landing awkwardly on her pillows and finding little comfort.

Her breathing had grown shallow and rapid, and she knew she could not move herself from that spot. In truth, she dared not try, for fear she would set off a fit of coughing. Laying awkwardly on her back as she was, Diana was suddenly so afraid that she would cough up blood that she would choke on it in that position, for she was entirely unable to help herself. She was slowly seized by a mortal panic and wondered at it. Just days before, when she had coughed herself to a point at which she could no longer breathe, she had almost given in to death. Diana had almost welcomed it and wondered at the peace it might finally give her.

And yet, just days later, the very prospect terrified her. Perhaps it was just the manner of her death which had her so very troubled? Perhaps, deep down, she would rather float away peacefully from lack of breath than drown in her own blood unable to even raise herself up and call for help.

As she continued to lay there, Diana began to feel terribly cold. She could feel her feet beginning to turn numb as they were exposed to the cooler air. The fire was roaring away in the grate, but it was not enough for somebody as sick as she to be able to go uncovered for any length of time.

Of course, Diana knew that she would not be left alone without the attendance of one her maids. It was simply a case of remaining calm and waiting patiently. In truth, she could only have but minutes to lay there before one of them came in to check upon her. They were most attentive to their mistress, and Diana could not find any fault with them whatsoever.

Deciding to take her mind off her own ragged breathing and the fear of coughing, Diana thought back just a few short years to when she and her grandmother were in the middle of one of the greatest marriage plots imaginable.

Diana had done what she could to hide her trepidation at the idea of marrying the wayward Prince of Wales. Fearing that she had hurt her grandmother with so vehement an expression of concern, Diana did what she could to give the impression she had warmed greatly to the idea and was, in fact, greatly excited by it. In truth, it had not been an easy thing for her to do.

All the while, Diana had tried to content herself with the idea that being a princess would be a marvellous thing. It would be the realisation of every woman's dream, and she had much to be grateful to her grandmother for.

"Grandmother, is our plan yet known to King George and Queen Caroline?" Diana had asked, still worried that her grandmother had not given her the full facts.

"He is, in essence, estranged from his parents. If he chooses to marry without informing them, that is his own business, is it not?"

"I cannot think that this will work, Grandmother. After all, is King George not given to such tremendous rages as to kick his coat and wig about the floor in anger? I fear what will happen to us all if we go ahead with this thing if it is so far against the king's wishes."

"I do not believe he has any wishes at all for his son," The Dowager Duchess said and shrugged. "It is true that the relationship between them has never been repaired since their abandonment of him all those years ago. I have even heard it said that Queen Caroline detests her eldest child and wishes him dead."

"Good Heavens, can that be true?" Diana felt suddenly better disposed towards Frederick. What must it feel like to have one's own parent wish them out of this earthly realm?

"It is spoken of quite openly at court, I

believe. There is great animus between the King and Queen and their eldest son. They make no secret that they favour his younger brother, William."

"And yet it is their eldest son who will take the throne when finally King George II dies. Surely they still would like to give authority to whomever it is he chooses to marry."

"I wish you would not worry so, my dear little Di. You will very soon be a princess, and nothing will be able to take that away from you once it is done. Once you and Prince Frederick are married and your marriage is consummated, there is nobody who can break that, not even the King himself."

The Dowager Duchess of Marlborough had such a way of putting things and spoke in such strident and confident tones that Diana had finally been carried along with the whole thing. After all, her grandmother had been the main beacon of safety and security in her life, and she had always known what to do. Why would Diana ever believe that her grandmother would lead her wrong in anything?

"And has the Prince himself really agreed to our wedding?" Diana asked, still rather unable to believe that a Prince of the Realm truly wanted her hand in marriage.

"He most certainly has, Di. In truth, I have never seen a man so determined and set upon his path. I have never seen a man keener to march towards matrimony than that man is."

"And you think he regards me well, Grandmother?"

"Of course, he regards you well, child. What man in his right senses and with his own eyes would not regard you well?"

"You flatter me, Grandmother, I am sure of it. But I shall accept your compliments with as much love as they are given." Diana laughed.

"And I hope you shall always continue to do so." The Dowager laughed also.

"So, tell me, when am I to be married?" Diana said, finally allowing herself a little excitement at the prospect.

After all, Prince Frederick was a handsome enough man, and the idea of marrying a prince was, perhaps, just a little exciting when all was said and done.

"You are to be married just a few weeks from now, my dear. The date is set between the Prince and me, and I shall let you have it very soon. It is to be kept as secret as possible, you see."

"In case the King hears of it?"

"In case *anybody* who would object

hears of it. We have come too far to have external interference disrupt our plans now, Diana."

"And is everything to be secret from me? Am I not the bride, after all?" Diana said, pettishly.

"Well, I can tell you this much. Your wedding shall take place in the Lodge at Windsor Great Park. The venue, of course, is also a secret, my dear. However much excitement you might feel in light of all that is about to happen to you, you must not breathe a word to anybody. You must keep it entirely to yourself. Confide in nobody, no female friends nor any servant. Everything about this is to stay tightly between us all, and that way we shall reach our goal in the end."

"The Lodge at Windsor Great Park," Diana said, doubtfully.

The Dowager Duchess had been the appointed Ranger of Windsor Great Park in the time of Queen Anne and, despite her relational difficulties with her old friend, Sarah Churchill maintained the role and continued it into the reign of the Hanoverians. As such, she had the use of the Lodge as a home whenever she chose it. It had been the place in which her beloved husband had died, and she had, after so many years, come almost to think of the building as truly one of her own homes.

"Why do you look so doubtful, my dear?"

"It is just that the Lodge is, ostensibly, yours. If somebody were to catch wind of this plot at all, would that not be one place they would seek us all out?"

"If we all behave and resist the temptation to make any talk whatsoever of this marriage, then there shall be none who will know and none to come looking. I do wish you would not worry quite so much about it all, Di."

"I am sorry to be so worried about it, Grandmother, I just do not want your hard work to come to nought. I know what it means to you to have me married to the very best, and I know what you have gone through to seize this opportunity for me."

"Then I would beg that you worry no further. As much as we are having to keep these things a secret, there is no reason why you should not look forward to your forthcoming nuptials with anything other than girlish excitement. Just think of it, you are about to become a princess, married to a man who will one day be the most powerful man in the land. That is all that you should think about, Diana. That is what you must concentrate upon."

Diana's breathing had returned to normal, although she was still too weak to move herself. In truth, the cold had begun to creep deep into her very bones and had become her greatest concern at that moment once the threat of choking had passed. However, as predicted, one of her trusty maids soon appeared and, full of distress seeing her mistress laid out in such a manner, she exclaimed effusively and hurriedly set The Duchess of Bedford to rights.

"Oh, Your Grace. How cold you feel. I shall stoke the fire a little higher still." The maid was entirely flustered, her face stricken and panicked.

"You have nothing to fear, my dear girl," Diana said, keen that the kind young woman should not make herself so uneasy about everything. "I shall soon warm very nicely now that the covers are upon me again. And in truth, the entire thing was my own fault. I had taken it into my mind that I would rise to my feet and take a turn about the room. When it came to it, I had only strength enough to free myself from my linens and bedspread. Once that was done, I found myself shattered."

"Your Grace, I should have helped you had I known."

"I know, my dear," Diana said, kindly. "You would perhaps have done a little better for me and begged that I would not try to rise to my feet in the first place, as would be entirely sensible." Diana laughed, and her maid nervously laughed with her.

"Your Grace, I shall go and have a hot beef tea prepared for you. Once that is inside your belly that will warm you from head to toe." The maid smiled weakly and bobbed a small curtsy before leaving the room.

"How very kind," Diana said, not hearing how vague and almost distant her voice sounded.

Left to herself once again, Diana could not help but return to the marriage plot and follow it through in her mind to its very conclusion.

Finally, her grandmother had given her the date that she was to be wed, and she had made every preparation that she needed to in complete secrecy. With just days to go before the nuptials were due to take place, the Dowager Duchess of Marlborough was seized with a rage the like of which Diana had never seen.

"I will find out who has done this if it takes me until I draw my last breath!" Sarah Churchill had roared as she paced the floor of the drawing-room. Her exclamation had been so very loud that Diana, who was finishing a late breakfast several rooms away, heard her clearly.

She had seen her grandmother frustrated and furious before but never had she seen her overcome by such a vile anger. Diana was so terrified that she almost did not run to find her grandmother for fear of what she would find. However, her deep love and admiration for the woman very soon replaced the fear, and Diana found herself suddenly concerned for her dearest relative.

Rising from the dining table, Diana set off for the drawing-room at a running pace.

"Grandmother, whatever has happened?" Diana said breathlessly the very moment she entered the drawing room.

"We have been discovered! We have been discovered!" The Dowager's face was scarlet with rage.

"Grandmother, I beg you, please sit down," Diana said, feeling her voice tremble and knowing herself to be on the verge of frightened tears.

"That Robert Walpole will rue the day he crossed me! He has found me out and has put a stop to everything!"

"Grandmother, please, I cannot bear to see you in such a way. You are frightening me, and I am so worried that you are going to have a fit or even worse." Diana was crying openly and could feel her hands shaking terribly. "I beg you would sit down."

As Diana's frightened tears continued to flow, her grandmother continued to pace. With her face growing ever redder, it was clear that the ageing Dowager had no intention of taking a rest or keeping her wild emotions in check. It was at that moment that Lady Diana Spencer realised what a truly formidable woman her grandmother really was. This was not rhetoric, or an anecdotal tale told years after an event. This was a very determined woman in full flight, and Diana no longer wondered how it was that her grandmother had made such a success of her own life and those around her. She no longer wondered how it was that her grandmother was one of the wealthiest people in the country.

"Grandmother, what has been found out? Is it the wedding?" Diana asked, still crying but keen to engage her grandmother in conversation rather than letting her continue to pace and rant.

"Of course, it is the wedding, child." the Dowager said angrily. "Oh, do forgive me, my dear little Di. I would not snap at you for all the world."

As Diana's tears became outright sobs, her grandmother seemed finally to regain control of her senses. Striding across the room, she very quickly gathered her granddaughter into her arms and held her tightly.

"Forgive me, child. Forgive me," she

whispered over and over again into Diana's thick fair hair.

"There is nothing to forgive, Grandmother. I am just worried that you will injure yourself if you continue. Please, just tell me what has happened."

"I shall do as you say, child." The Dowager drew in a deep breath, and Diana rather thought she had never heard her grandmother speak such words before.

"And you will sit, will you not?" Diana took her grandmother's hands and squeezed them tightly.

"I shall sit, child."

"And I shall have some tea sent in," Diana said, kissing her grandmother's cheek, her own face still wet with tears.

The Dowager Duchess did not wait. "Robert Walpole has found us out, Diana." The

Dowager sniffed miserably. "He has discovered my plan that you and the Prince of Wales should marry and he has put an end to it."

"By speaking with the King?"

"Yes, I daresay he has spoken with him at length."

"But are we quite safe, Grandmother?"

"Of course, we are, my dear little Di. The King has simply disallowed it, that is all. We are in no danger for ourselves."

"But how came Robert Walpole to know it all?" Diana asked, feeling a little guilty that she felt a secret stab of relief. She was not to marry Prince Frederick after all. She was never to be a princess, and she could not entirely say that she was sorry. Of course, Diana knew that she could not voice such things to her redoubtable grandmother, especially when that fine woman had fought so hard to secure her favourite granddaughter the very best in life.

"Walpole has his spies everywhere. They infest the corridors of power like rats. They crawl about Parliament, and they creep about the Royal household. If only the Prince of Wales had kept his own counsel." The Dowager shook her head from side to side in a mixture of disbelief and frustration.

"So, the Prince made it known?" Diana said incredulously.

"Of course he has, for neither you nor I have done it. The Prince has spoken out of turn, likely when he was too far in his cups! The fool!"

"He must have, Grandmother, for I swear to you that I have never uttered a word of it," Diana said, feeling guilty despite the fact that she was telling the absolute truth.

"I know you have not my dear, sweet Diana. Unfortunately, a man who drinks is also a man who talks." She sighed.

Diana could not help but wonder what sort of a life she might truly have had being married to a man who took too much alcohol. Again, her sentiment would remain silent; unspoken.

"And what is it to Robert Walpole? What stake has he in the marriage of the Prince of Wales?" Diana knew that she was speaking as if she were a most naïve young woman. Her grandmother knew as well as she did that Diana had a firm grasp of politics and the machinations of those who practised its darker arts.

Robert Walpole had been the First Lord of the Treasury and had become the first so-called Prime Minister in 1721. Despite the fact that Walpole and the Dowager Duchess were both Whigs, they had a long-standing, deep mistrust of one another. Furthermore, Walpole had favoured peace in Europe, whereas the Dowager had not. There never seemed a point upon which the pair could agree.

"He wants a marriage between the Prince of Wales and Augusta of Saxe-Gotha. He is most determined to see it done and he has influence enough to see it brought about."

"Saxe-Gotha?" Diana mused. "The daughter of the Duke of Saxe-Gotha?"

"Yes. She can be no more than eleven or twelve years. Still, I know Walpole well enough to know he will wait to get what he wants. He wants an alliance, you see. For diplomatic reasons, Walpole wants a union with a Duchy of the Holy Roman Empire."

"So, it is not done, then?"

"It is as good as done." The Dowager

shook her head angrily. "Walpole will work on the King, who will no doubt see some benefit in the plan."

"But what of the Prince of Wales?"

"Oh, he will simply go along with it all."

"But they are a family estranged. He has no love for his parents, and he has gone against them in all other ways. I cannot see how they will get him to comply?"

"Can you not? He is a young man of many debts and rich tastes. They need only offer him a greater allowance than that which he currently enjoys."

"And you think he would take it?"

"I know he would take it, Diana."

"So, he is not a man of great character after all?"

"No, but with your direction, he would have been. I had every confidence in your ability to mould him, my dear little Di... otherwise, I should not have embarked upon the thing in the first place."

"So, I am not to marry a prince after all," Diana said quite neutrally. Whilst she felt sad for the demise of her grandmother's efforts, she did not truly feel sad for herself.

"No, my dear, you are not to marry a prince." The Dowager took a great breath. "And I really am so very sorry."

"You have nothing to be sorry for, Grandmother," Diana said and raced to her grandmother's side where she dropped to her knees by her chair. "You have striven to do the very best for me and find the very best match you could possibly find. It matters not that it did not come to fruition, my dear Grandmother; what matters more than anything is how you tried. I shall never forget what you have done for me, and I shall never forget the great pains you have taken to find me a life far from ordinary."

"You are such a good girl, Diana," the Dowager Duchess said as she wearily placed a hand upon her granddaughters bowed head. "And I would have given anything to make you a princess, my dear. Anything in this world."

"I know you would have, Grandmother."

As the maid came in carrying the hot beef tea that she had promised, Diana wondered at the fact that her old feelings still had the ability to fill her with guilt. And yet, what good would that do? The marriage plot had come to nought, and it was not because of her own cautious feeling on the matter. It has come to nought because the Prime Minister had discovered it and broken it. The fault did not lie with Diana, and she finally needed to let go of such ideas.

Diana had never hurt her grandmother with her feelings on the subject, and never would. The thing was done now, never to be revisited again.

Chapter Nine

"You still look unwell, my dear. Am I to take it that the physician's diagnosis of tuberculosis stands?" John Russell, the Duke of Bedford, had pulled a chair towards her bed, taking care that he does not find himself too close.

"It still stands, John. Although, I ought to tell you that there is only any danger when I am coughing. If I am not coughing or sneezing, then you are quite safe." Diana could not hide her annoyance at her husband's distance from her.

"But what of your pregnancy? I have heard nothing of it since I returned to Woburn Abbey."

"The pregnancy, if ever there was one, no longer exists. I am not yet convinced that my early symptoms were those of pregnancy and not the early signs of this tuberculosis." Diana knew that she did not speak the truth entirely. In her heart, she had known, and she had been more sure of her pregnancy than she had ever been of anything.

The news that the baby was gone was a dark hole inside of her. And yet she knew that she must handle this diplomatically and the very thought exhausted her more than she could say. Instead of being able to grieve the loss of her child she must pander to convention and this man who had never loved her.

"Well, I suppose we shall never know, shall we?" The Duke of Bedford said, shortly. "But if you were pregnant, it rather looks as if, yet again, you did not take due care of yourself."

"Due care of myself?" Diana said, her eyes filling with tears at the injustice of his comments. "I did not contract tuberculosis on a whim, John. Nobody could or would do such a thing."

"But you did not take care *not* to contract it."

"And in what manner might I have achieved such a thing, John? When tuberculosis has its moment and runs wildly through our country, tell me what else I ought to have done?"

"As always, you were out and about. You never keep home if you can possibly spend time with that grandmother of yours. If you had not been out and about so much, you might never have contracted it. This might not have happened, and I might finally, have an heir."

"I remember a time when you simply wanted a child, John, and were not so fixated upon an heir," Diana spoke quietly as her tears continued to fall.

Having been hurt by her husband's return to Woburn Abbey when first she had gone to Southampton House, now as she regarded him some feet away from her bedside, Diana would have wished him anywhere else on earth. Even now, as she suffered an illness the like of which she had never suffered in her life, her own husband could not set aside his disappointments.

How could he not see that her own losses were equal to his, and even more heartfelt, for they had to do with being a mother and not with producing an heir?

When first she had been married to John, he had simply been Lord John Russell. It was his elder brother who had been the Duke of Bedford, and John had simply been excited at the idea of them having a child of their own. Of course, as with all men of title, he was undoubtedly keen for a son. However, the mania and determination to produce a child had not been evident then.

In truth, Diana had thought them somewhat happy in the early days, although it was a happiness which had been rather short lived.

Just a few short months after the failed attempt at marriage with the Prince of Wales, Diana became very sensible of a feeling of panic, or at least urgency, which seemed to radiate from the Dowager Duchess of Marlborough. Almost as if she sensed that the plot, should it become known, would have somehow damaged her granddaughter's chances for a good match, Sarah Churchill seemed to rather settle upon the young Lord Russell, with the idea that he would, somehow, become the Duke of Bedford.

"I do not know how you can be sure of

such a thing, Grandmother," Diana had said with a laugh when first the Dowager Duchess had raised the subject. "His brother is but three years older and still a young man."

"I have a feeling about the current Duke of Bedford. I do not believe Wriothesley Russell to be long for this world."

"Grandmother, what a thing to say!" Diana had said, although she could not help but laugh at her grandmother's typical attempt at forward planning.

"There is an air about him. An air of sickness."

"Then it is something that we should be sorry for, Grandmother, not something that we should wish for." Diana chastised her grandmother, but only in a playful manner. In truth, she would never have dared to scold her grandmother for anything.

"No indeed, but it does make John Russell a little more appealing, does it not?"

"He would seem to be rather appealing in his own right, Grandmother," Diana said with a shy smile. "For he is handsome, is he not?"

"He is handsome enough, child, but handsomeness cannot always be trusted. It is title and power which can always be relied upon, for it never loses its appeal as time weighs down upon it."

"Indeed," Diana said, acquiescing as she shook her head a little and laughed. "Although it is true that I do not know him particularly well."

"I have heard no gossip to suggest that he is anything other than respectable, my dear, if that is your current worry. And if he is soon to be the Duke of Bedford, and he is as young as you are yourself, he shall easily be moulded by you. And I, of course, shall use my influence to raise him up in some manner or other. Likely politics or something similar."

"You are always thinking of everything, Grandmother. You never leave anything to chance, do you?" Diana said wistfully.

"Do you remember what I told you about chance, my dear? It is called chance for a reason, and I do not trust it."

"And you are keen for me to marry him?"

"Indeed, I am, my dear little Di, but I should be happier still to know that you are keen to marry him for yourself. It is, perhaps, not such a great union as the one between yourself and the Prince of Wales might have been, but there is nothing now that I can do to change that."

"I have no regrets about that business, Grandmother, beyond the regrets that you worked so hard to have your plan come to nought. As far as Lord John Russell is concerned, I should be glad enough to be married to him, whether he finally becomes the Duke of Bedford or not."

"My dear Diana, you ought really to be a little more ambitious than that. Whilst we have had to settle for this young man in many regards, you must maintain hope that he will reach a higher station still. The higher he reaches, my dear, the higher you reach. It is all that I want for you in this world."

And so it was, on 11th October 1731, Lady Diana Spencer married Lord John Russell.

The early weeks of the marriage had gone tremendously well, and Diana had felt herself to have a curious sort of freedom that she had never felt before. She was suddenly the mistress of her own home, with nobody to defer to in the duties and responsibilities which that particular role entailed.

Not that Diana had ever, for one moment, resented her grandmother's great role and influence in her life. The truth was that she missed her grandmother's company greatly and did everything she could to see her as often as possible. When the two could not be together, Diana wrote to her at least twice a week, if not three times. Always her grandmother responded in kind and seemed for all the world to be missing her granddaughter as much as her granddaughter was missing her.

In the spring of 1732, just months after they were married, Lady Diana Russell discovered that she was expecting her first child.

Keeping the information to herself for a few short days, Diana could not help but enjoy the sweetest secret she had ever kept. She was to be a mother and, knowing that a life existed inside her own belly, Diana knew that she had never wanted anything more in her entire life. For days on end, she imagined herself cradling her child and watching him grow into a handsome little boy, and then a very fine young man. Of course, if the child were to be a girl, Diana would do what she could to raise her with a similar influence to that she herself had enjoyed in the heart of her grandmother's home.

"And you are sure? You have seen the physician?"

When first Diana had told John of the news, she detected the purest joy in his countenance.

"I have seen the physician, John, and it is as sure as it can be. We are expecting a child, my dear, and I shall pray that I produce a son for you."

"Well, what fine news this is!" John rose to his feet and embraced his wife. "What a clever young woman you are."

Pregnancy for Lady Diana Russell had been a rather mixed set of experiences, much as it was for many women of the era. She had her petty maladies and other complaints, coupled with moments of extreme radiance and wellness and great joy. Finally settled in a successful marriage with a child on the way, all that there was left for Lady Diana Russell to do was to patiently await the birth of her baby.

Chapter Ten

My Dearest Grandmother,

I thank you kindly for your warm and unwavering attention to me these last weeks at Southampton House. Your visits have been a great source of strength to me, and I cannot possibly ever convey the depth of my gratitude to you.

I have, as I believe you are aware, been dwelling much in reminiscence of late. But I have reached a stage in my history where there is nothing of good to be found, and yet I cannot help but go over it all. I remember you telling me that reminiscences are not always healthy, and finally I believe you spoke the truth that day.

However, it rather seems that reminiscences cannot be stopped in their tracks, nor even turned away from for a moment.

Whilst I know that you will be back with me in a day or two, I cannot lay here without setting down everything that I am feeling. By committing it to paper, it is almost as if you are here with me now, consoling me the way you always do and blessing me with your loving kindness.

This last day I have found myself going over and over the worst reminiscence of my life. Already I perceive that you will know what is coming, and yet I must set it all down here once more.

I talk, of course, of that day in early November 1732 when I was returning home in my carriage. The horse had taken fright and had somehow or other, I still do not know the facts, managed to turn the carriage over. In truth, the only thing I remember of it all was seeming to take flight almost like a bird as I was first thrown against the door and then thrown out of the carriage altogether. Beyond that, I remember nothing else.

I remember no pain or fear at the time of the accident, simply blackness and nothingness. I remember very little of my immediate treatment and convalescence, and nothing of note until that day, just days after the accident, when I began an early labour.

I knew that my baby was going to be born terribly early and, as I began to give birth to him, I could do nothing but fear for his life. He had not yet been due for many weeks, and I was so worried that he would be too little to survive in this world. Of course, my worst fears were born out as true.

My child was born, baptised, and died in one day. Poor little John, the Marquis of

Tavistock for just one day.

And yet I did not know it, of course. Although I have not told you much of this time, I must tell it to you now. I had been so very ill following the accident and my subsequent labour that, following what was deemed to be a grand consultation, it was decided that I should not immediately be told of my own child's death.

I was to be fooled and hoodwinked until the moment all around me thought me to be well enough and strong enough to be told the truth.

In furtherance of this, doubtless, kindly meant plan, every day an infant boy was brought to me to look at. He was fetched in by one of the maids and shown to me for a few moments here and there since I was deemed too weak and too unwell to hold and nurse him myself.

In truth, he was the reason that I likely rallied as quickly as I did, for I felt I had a son whom I must get well for in order that I could be a good mother to him. Little did I know that my own child was gone and I would never see him. Little did I know that the tiny pink baby boy they fetched to me every day was nothing more than an unwitting pretender. He was not mine, nor would he ever be.

My own boy was dead, and I had never been able to be a mother to him. I had never been able to hold him.

I cannot think of those days without such a tumult of emotions. Whatever argument I have now with my husband, I feel sure that he acted in my best interest at the time. However, those very best of interests damaged me more than anything ever could have. They gave me a hope that was not mine, and a child I no longer had.

There is no way to describe to you the desolation I felt when finally they told me the truth. I did not have a son... and had not had a son for any more than one day. He had died as a direct result of my having been thrown from the carriage just days before.

I think the worst thing of all for me was the fact that I had not known. I had always imagined, especially throughout the time of my pregnancy, that being a mother would somehow give me instincts above and beyond those I already possessed. How could my son really have died? Surely I would have known it? Surely I would have felt it in the very core of my being?

And when the baby pretender had been presented to me day after day, how had I not recognised him as such? How had I not known and instantly recognised him as simply a child of another woman? It is that feeling, more than any other, that I simply cannot shake, however hard I try. I could not help but feel that I had failed my son, not least by not being strong enough to prevent his death, but by not recognising his death when it occurred.

For day after day, I simply lay in my bed desolate. It was strange, but I could not help but think of Judith Tichborne, my father's third wife.

I could not help but think of that very first time she had lost a child, long before even it had been due to be born. I thought back to my young self and how much I lacked understanding of the situation. And yet, I had understood her desperate cries on an instinctive level. Judith had experienced the greatest pain a woman can experience, and she went on to experience it again and again.

Perhaps I ought to have been grateful that my first child had at least drawn breath; had at least lived out his first day when poor

Judith's had not even opened his eyes in this world. And yet, despite it all, I could feel nothing but pain and anguish. I could find no circumstance about which to be grateful, either on my account or that of my son.

I have thought of Judith often since those days following my own loss, and find myself pleased that she has finally given birth to a child who has survived this world thus far. Once again, she has been married to a man who is so much her senior, and yet it would seem to be her lot in life. I can only hope and pray that the loss of children is not also her lot in life, for I would not wish that on anybody in this world, not even the worst of my enemies.

Of course, Grandmother, the loss of baby John was a great source of pain to my husband also. Whatever has passed between us in the days which have followed, I cannot deny him his grief. It was a grief which was true and terrible to witness and, for some time hence, we could hardly speak to each other for fear of the emotions that would easily rise to the surface.

Those were the hardest of days, and I should never wish to repeat them. I do not care even to think of them, and yet I cannot seem able to stop myself. Perhaps if I write it all down to you here and now it will be done. Perhaps it will not catch me unawares in whatever time I have left, but rather it might leave me in peace for just a while.

And then, of course, there came the news that my husband, John, had finally become the Duke of Bedford, just as you had predicted he would, Grandmother. Wriothesley Russell had apparently died in Corunna in Spain on the 23rd October 1732 at the age of just four and twenty. And yet we had not heard of it until well into November.

My husband had already been a Duke, had he but known it, when he lost his son and heir. Above all things, I think that has affected him very greatly. In many respects, it overtook and overshadowed the pain of a very human loss. It transformed it into something quite different, something quite other.

I cannot say which has changed my husband the most; becoming the Duke of Bedford, or losing his first-born son. Perhaps it is a mixture of the two things, but that is something that I can never know.

You had said, Grandmother, that if my husband became a Duke as a young man, then he would be easy to mould. Perhaps that might have been true had we never lost our first child. I really do believe that our first year of marriage was as happy as any marriage can be in its infancy. We were still coming to know each other, and I do believe that we both of us liked what it was we were finding out about the other.

I think I know in my heart that we can never return to those early days, for too much has happened. We have each of us lost too much, and we have somehow chosen to bear our loss separately rather than together. Perhaps if we had learned how to bear our losses together, then we might not be apart this very day.

Once again, my husband is returned to Woburn Abbey, and I do not know when he shall come back. There are days when I wish I would never see him again; the days when he is particularly cruel in his words. And then, there are the other days; the days in which I long for him to be here. The days in which I long for things to return to the way they were before loss and grief once again overshadowed my life.

I cannot help but look back over all the

years of my life and see how it is liberally peppered with the loss and grieving for loved ones. On that day nineteen years ago when I had my first taste of bereavement, the day I lost my own dear mother, my young self could never have imagined how many more losses were to come.

And now, at just five and twenty years, I cannot help but think that I have lost more people than I have managed to keep close to me, and I cannot help but wonder if my life is to continue in this vein.

Am I simply to expect that my years be filled with pain and sorrow? Or is the next loss truly to be the one I have come to dread? The loss of myself. And yet, if everything that my dear sister, Anne, told me all those years ago is correct, then all those I have lost shall be waiting for me in Heaven.

That would be a very fine day for me,

would it not? To find myself suddenly free of pain and sadness and reunited in the arms of all those I have loved and lost.

I cannot help but think that the years I spent with you in your adoption were the safest and most pain-free of my life. Whilst we lost Grandfather early on in that period, we went many long years, did we not, without the sort of grief that I had experienced before and after our time together.

My dear Grandmother, I have so much to thank you for. You looked after me so well, and you kept me safe from life's pain and sorrow, although how you managed it, I do not quite know. However, knowing you as well as I do, I know that you can manage any situation and make it work. That is your gift, my dear Dowager Duchess.

Again, I turn my attention to John and wonder if he shall make it back before I am too weak to receive him. He said nothing of when he is due to return from Woburn Abbey, although I am sure that he would come if I could find the courage to write to him. Perhaps I shall do that, and perhaps I shall not.

I remember once saying to you that I was pleased to marry John Russell whether he finally became a Duke or not. You told me then that I ought to have more ambition, and yet I shall say that I now wish he had never made his title. Had his brother never died that day in Spain, we would both certainly have been spared the desperate mania for an heir to be produced between us. For in truth, it has not just hurt me.

I very much believe that it has hurt John also in ways that he yet cannot, and probably will never, understand. It has taken something from him, and it is something that he will never get back. It has taken his right to ordinary grief somehow and turned what should be a pure display of pain and sorrow into a rather ugly anger and disappointment. It is this anger and disappointment which stops him truly following the path of grief and walking steadfastly upon it until he reaches its end. In my heart, I fear he will never reach that point, and will always feel as he does at this moment.

However, the days in which we conversed with each other with the ease of a happy husband and wife are already several years behind us. In truth, they had only really just begun when the first of our tragedies struck.

Perhaps, rather than feeling so very hurt by his words, I should put my efforts into praying for his own peace of mind and find my own peace of mind in forgiving him. And perhaps I ought really to try to achieve this one thing before it is too late.

Forgive me my melancholy, my dear Grandmother, but I feel dreadfully alone here today. Of course, I know I shall see you very soon, perhaps even before you receive this letter, but still, I have to know it is on its way to you. Still, I have to know, at this moment, that I have you to talk to, whether you are here or not.

With the greatest of love,

your affectionate granddaughter,

Diana.

Chapter Eleven

Diana's maid had helped her seal her letter and had immediately made to dispatch it. However, the writing down of such fraught emotions had exhausted Diana entirely and, as she tried to make herself comfortable in her bed, she was seized with yet another fit of coughing. This time, the blood came fast and immediate, and she had no time or even the energy to cover her mouth at all.

Diana had not yet seen so much blood expelled from her lungs, and she could not help but think that surely this signalled that her own life must soon be drawing to its conclusion. She was not getting better, rather she was getting worse and worse, fading day by day, her already thin body being entirely consumed by the tuberculosis.

Her maid helped her as best she could and, in no time at all, had made her mistress comfortable. Sending out for help, she and two other maids had quickly replaced the blood-soaked bed linens and their mistress' spoiled nightgown.

Determining that the physician would be sent for immediately, one of the younger maids remained quietly in the corner of the room, refusing to leave her mistress even as she slept.

Diana, feeling greatly comforted simply by the presence of another human being, lay still in her bed, too weak to even turn over into another position. She let her mind drift back to thoughts of her recovery after the death of her first child.

In the weeks that followed the horror of the carriage accident and all the pain and suffering it brought with it, Diana Russell wondered if she would ever recover. She and her new husband seemed to grow apart so very quickly, becoming almost strangers to each other.

Except, of course, they were not strangers at night. His new and unexpected role as Duke, coupled with the grief of losing his first child, had changed John considerably. His desperation for an heir became rather manic, and he seemed to find a great urgency in the idea that his wife should conceive almost immediately.

With her heart truly broken and her life finally feeling as if it had been shattered, Diana had been forced to turn her attention to the conception of another child. She must accept her husband, night after night, whatever her own torn feelings. Without time to heal both physically and mentally from the trauma she had suffered, Diana found herself growing to hate the attentions of the Duke of Bedford. She wanted time to grieve and time to heal, and he would afford her neither of those things.

Just months after baby John had died, the Duchess of Bedford was pregnant once more.

"Are you absolutely sure?" Although John seemed pleased, in fact, happier than she had seen him those past months, still something about his form of jubilation felt very different; almost wrong.

When Diana had delivered the news, her husband had held her very briefly and, as he spoke, she could not help but compare their minor celebration with that they had shared when she had become pregnant for the first time.

She knew that it was tainted. It was in no way the same pureness of feeling that they had both felt that very first time. It was, instead, a pleasure for very different reasons. For John Russell, it was the idea that his efforts and determination for an heir had finally been rewarded. For Diana, it was simply that she had managed to conceive and please her husband and do her duty.

Throughout those first weeks of her new pregnancy, Diana had felt most dreadfully unwell. In truth, her body had not yet recovered from the accident and her previous labour, not to mention the anguish and self-neglect which had followed the loss of baby John. She was by no means a healthy woman at that stage, and there had been none of the radiance or high points of pregnancy that she had previously experienced. All in all, she had simply felt ill and exhausted for much of the time.

When, just weeks after announcing her pregnancy, Diana miscarried, she had not been entirely surprised. Devastated, yes, but surprised she had not been. She had known herself to feel unwell and had known herself by no means strong enough to carry her child to full term. But then, she had not been well enough at the time of conception, and despite her best efforts, had not been able to control the will of mother nature, however much she had tried to.

"I can hardly believe you have lost the second of my children, Diana." Before she had even had a chance to recover, John had greatly accused her.

"I am so terribly sorry, John. I do not understand what it is you think I could have done about it. I did not lose my child on purpose, and my heart is broken for the second time."

"I do not wish to cause you any further pain, my dear wife, but I cannot help but say that this might not have happened had you looked after yourself better. You should have paid better attention to your own health and well-being, for that is truly the only way to secure a safe and successful birth."

"I did not make myself unwell, John. I was simply unwell anyway. I had not recovered from the events of last year, and yet you would persist in seeing that I conceived at the earliest opportunity. I cannot take the blame for that."

"It is your duty to provide me with an heir, Diana. In order to do that, it is your duty to look after yourself."

John had left his admonishment of her at that, never once apologising for the harshness of his words or the effect his words might have had on a woman who had just lost her second child.

It was to be another two years before Diana fell pregnant again, despite the Duke of

Bedford's determination and best efforts.

Diana's morning sickness had been unlike any she had experienced during her first two pregnancies, being much more pronounced and debilitating. When finally she had announced to her husband that they were expecting for the third time, he had simply nodded his approval. There had been no contact, no comfort, nor any congratulations.

"Well, it is incumbent upon you to look after yourself now, Diana. Is a pregnant woman not supposed to put weight on? I must say, it very much looks to me as if you are losing weight and not gaining as you should. I must insist now that you eat properly and rest as necessary. Health is your primary duty over these next months, Diana, and I expect you to perform your duty, do you understand?"

"Yes, John, I understand."

Within days of her announcement, Diana knew that there was something terribly wrong. Try as she might to eat everything she could manage, still, she lost weight. Furthermore, she developed the most dreadful cough and seemed unable to shake it. As the days passed, she became more and more exhausted, and her exhaustion was weakening her to a point where she could barely stand. Finally, when first she had coughed blood into her crisp white handkerchief, a physician had been called. In seemingly no time at all, he had diagnosed tuberculosis.

Diana had taken to her bed in Woburn Abbey and had begged that her grandmother be sent for. Seeing how very ill her granddaughter was, the Dowager Duchess of Marlborough immediately tackled the Duke of Bedford, forcing him to have Diana moved to Southampton House, his home in Bloomsbury Square. That way she would have easier access to her beloved granddaughter and not have to travel out to Bedfordshire to see her. Furthermore, she would be able to seek out the very finest physicians that London had to offer.

Diana had not been at Southampton House but a matter of days before she knew that she was no longer pregnant.

Diana was mercifully pulled back into the present when her maid hurriedly rose to her feet at the sudden appearance of the Dowager Duchess of Marlborough.

"My dear Grandmother, I had just this afternoon written you a letter and had it sent out to you."

"Well, I am here now, my child."

"It is rather a sad and maudlin sort of letter, Grandmother, but I felt I must write it. It speaks of many feelings I have not truly shared before now, and I wonder if I could only ever have shared them in ink upon paper."

"Well, I see no need to be sad and maudlin at this time, my dear little Di. After all, I think you are looking rather better."

"No, Grandmother, I do not look better."

"My dear girl...."

"I am dying, Grandmother, you must know that by now." Diana sighed sadly.

"Please, do not say that, Diana. Do not say it for I cannot bear to hear it. I cannot bear to think about it."

"I know that I cannot go on much longer in this way. I have come to realise that I need to be released from all this pain, both physical and in my heart. I know now that I shall never be a mother, that I shall never fulfil my womanly destiny. Perhaps I ought to take some consolation from the fact that my husband will, undoubtedly, go on to sire the heir he has so very much wanted these last two years."

"I care not whether he goes on to sire an heir, Diana." At that moment, Diana saw the glimpse of the formidable woman her grandmother had always been, and it made her smile.

"I can always rely upon you to be so very strong, and you always have been. But you see, in these last days, I must find a way to forgive my husband."

"I am not sure that he deserves your forgiveness."

"In the end, we all deserve forgiveness. I know that John Russell has shown me nothing but disappointment in the loss of three babies, and yet I feel sure that he hurts in his own way. Perhaps registering his disappointment is a way of making his pain manifest. Perhaps it is the only way he is able to come to terms with all that he has lost; all that we both have lost."

"My dear Diana, I do love you so." A tear rolled down the Dowager Duchess' face, and it was the first that Diana had seen her grandmother cry for many years. "I am so very sorry."

"Of all people on this earth, Grandmother, you have nothing to be sorry for. You are the one person with whom I felt safe, and you have lavished me with more love and affection than perhaps any person has a right to receive.

You gave me everything that you had to give and more, and your hopes and dreams for me were endless if a little inventive at times." Diana smiled and was warmed to see that her grandmother smiled also.

"You deserved everything and more, Diana. I truly think that you are the only person in this world who has never disappointed me in any way whatsoever, and I thank you for that. You have been the most precious thing in my life, and I love you so dearly."

"And I love you too, Grandmother."

Epilogue

On 27th September 1735, Diana Russell, The Duchess of Bedford, formerly Lady Diana Spencer, died of tuberculosis in her chamber at Southampton House in Bloomsbury Square, London. She was just twenty-five-years-old. On 9th October, she was taken in a gun carriage to Chenies, Buckinghamshire, where she was laid to rest.

John Russell, the Duke of Bedford, went on to marry Lady Gertrude Leveson-Gower two years later. He finally sired the heir he had been so intent upon, and his son, Francis Russell, Marquis of Tavistock was born on 27th September 1739, four years to the day that

Diana had passed away.

However, his son and heir pre-deceased John Russell, dying in 1767, four years before the Duke.

John Russell's daughter, Lady Caroline Russell, grew up and married George Spencer, the 4th Duke of Marlborough.

Sarah Churchill, the Dowager Duchess of Marlborough, lived on for a further nine years beyond her dear little Di, passing away at the age of eighty-four at home in her beloved Marlborough House in 1744. She had outlived all her children. The house remained empty for several years thereafter before it finally became the property of the Dukes of Marlborough.

The Dowager Duchess was finally laid to rest at Blenheim Palace, with the exhumed body of her beloved husband, John Churchill, who had originally been buried at Westminster Abbey. They were joined together again as he was laid to rest beside her.

She never forgave John Russell for the death of her favourite granddaughter, volubly blaming the Duke for her sad demise.

Frederick, Prince of Wales, continued his affair with Anne Vane resulting in the birth of a son, Fitzfrederick Vane in 1732. The child died before his fourth birthday.

He fathered a second child with Anne in 1733, a daughter, Amelia, who died just one day after her birth.

In 1736, Frederick went on to father another child called Charles, this time with Margaret, Countess of Marsac. Charles lived to be eighty-four years old.

Finally, the Prince of Wales did exactly as Prime Minister Robert Walpole had desired and married the sixteen-year-old Augusta of Saxe-Gotha in 1736. He curtailed his philandering ways, if not his excessive spending, and otherwise settled down into the role of husband.

He continued to be at war with his parents, even spreading a rumour that his father, King George II was dying in 1737, when he had a bout of illness. His father soon recovered to full health.

It was also in 1737 that Augusta of Saxe-Gotha gave birth to their first child. They went on to have nine children in total, all of whom survived childhood.

In 1751, after reportedly being hit in the chest by a cricket ball, Prince Frederick died of what might well have been a pulmonary embolism.

His father, King George II, lived on for a further nine years, keeping the throne throughout the rest of his life.

The Prince of Wales never became the King that the Dowager Duchess of Marlborough predicted he would be.

In 1733, two years before the death of Diana, Henrietta Godolphin died. She was the eldest surviving daughter of the Duke and Duchess of Marlborough, and Diana's aunt.

When Henrietta's father, John Churchill, died in 1722 having no surviving male heir, the Dukedom passed to Henrietta, his eldest surviving daughter. An English Act of Parliament in 1706 had decreed that a 1st Duke could pass his title on to his eldest daughter if he had no son and, therefore, Henrietta, the 2nd Duchess of Marlborough was a Duchess in her own right rather than by marriage.

Henrietta died aged fifty-two. She had no surviving son to whom to pass the title and so it went to Diana's brother, Charles Spencer, who was then the 5th Earl of Sunderland.

The Hon. John Spencer, the youngest of Diana's brothers, inherited his father's estates in 1733. They ranged across three counties and included Althorpe in Northamptonshire.

He was married in 1733 and, in 1734, he fathered a son, also called John. It was this son who, in 1765 was given the titles Viscount Althorpe and the 1st Earl Spencer. His family retained Althorpe throughout the generations, and he is the direct ancestor of Lady Diana Spencer.

And so it was that more than two centuries later in 1961, a second Lady Diana Spencer was born. Named perhaps, after the first Diana, she also grew up to be a tall, fair, beautiful and compassionate young woman, all set to marry the Prince of Wales. This time, however, there was no need for secrecy and no need for a plot. On 29th July 1981, Lady Diana Spencer married the Price of Wales.

Sarah J Freeman

Author's Notes

I hope you enjoyed this account of the First Lady Diana Spencer and the tragedies that befell her. Though there are many records about her life and I have stuck to the facts as much as I could, I cannot guarantee that everything is factual. I have used what records are available and patched them together to give you as much knowledge and understanding as I can.

However, unlike the Princess Diana who was born in 1961, the one that we all know and love, the original Diana Spencer is not so well known and her life was not so well documented. As such, this book is a blending of historical fact and artistic licence. I have melded fact and fiction to allow you an inside view on what the characters must have been thinking.

I wanted to give you a peek into the drawing room of British life. I wanted you to feel as Diana felt through all her tragedies. It seems so sad to me that despite her vast wealth, she could not be saved from the loss of two children and the terrible tuberculosis. She could not be guaranteed a happy life. She did however, have the love and comfort of her grandmother and I know this would have been a great comfort to her.

Life in those times was harsh and difficult. Most women of title would not be given a choice of who they married and so much of Diana's story was not uncommon. I think she faced her challenges with courage and fortitude and I admire her for it. When I imagine how frightening it must have been to be married to a virtual stranger I wonder how I would have coped in her shoes.

Childbirth in the 1700's was very dangerous, both to the mother and to the child. Infant mortality rates were high. It is quoted that one in five or twenty percent of children would die before their second birthday.

In some districts, infant mortality was as high as seventy-five percent of all births. It has even been said that in the 1700's more people died in London than were baptised. Alongside these statistics, Diana's and her family's tragedies can no longer be seen as uncommon. This, however does not make the story less sad.

However, there were positives in her life. She had the constant companionship and mentorship of her grandmother. Her influence and love must have been a great comfort.

I hope you enjoyed this book and a look into the drawing-room of one of England's lesser known royals. I have really enjoyed researching the story of the beautiful and tragic first Lady Diana Spencer and a look into Georgian life.

Lady Diana Spencer 1710 – 1735

About the Author

Sarah J Freeman has always loved history but she always wanted more than the dry books and lectures she remembers from school. It intrigued her to know more about the historical characters. She wondered what they felt, and how they really lived. It is that curiosity that led to the writing of this book.

Sarah will be doing more books on interesting and exciting historical figures in the near future.

To find out who and when join her email list

http://eepurl.com/cD0299

for updates and occasional exclusive content.

You can interact with Sarah on **Facebook** by

searching for "**Sarah J Freeman**."

She will keep you up to date with all her new
releases.

Or you may email her via:

Fairhavensbooks@.cd2.com

Printed in Great Britain
by Amazon